100

The Suburban Captivity of the Churches

The Suburban Captivity of the Churches

AN ANALYSIS OF PROTESTANT RESPONSIBILITY

IN THE EXPANDING METROPOLIS

BY GIBSON WINTER

DOUBLEDAY & COMPANY, INC., GARDEN CITY, NEW YORK

1961

IN GRATITUDE TO THE PARISHFIELD COMMUNITY

Contents

Contents

Preface

The central concern of this book is the creation of a human environment in the metropolis. Can the metropolitan area become a suitable environment for human life? Are we to resign ourselves to a vicious circle of demolition, redevelopment, and spreading blight? Urban blight signifies the breakdown of human community before it becomes a physical problem; when men and women no longer *care*, no longer feel that they *belong*, their properties and neighborhoods disintegrate. The vicious circle is created when people who would have cared are driven from one blighted area into another until they no longer belong and cease to care; in time, their new area of residence will have to be demolished; meanwhile, the human resources of the society are bent and twisted.

The specific task of this study is to assess the role of the churches in the metropolis. The churches could play a significant role in metropolitan planning, and yet, for the most part, they have failed to participate responsibly in the metropolis. The writer has tried above all to clarify the nature of responsible participation, so that men and women in the churches may see the alternatives which confront them. Decisions made by religious bodies in the next decade could significantly alter the human environment of the metropolis. Church planning, as it is now called, implies planning *for* or *against* the metropolis as a human community; the building or removal of a church is a vote *for* or *against* the local neighborhood.

This evaluation began in 1955 when the Parishfield Community, a lay training center in Michigan, called together a group of specialists on urban problems to discuss the responsibility of the churches in the metropolis. After several years of consultations it became clear that glib answers would not meet the situation. The very conditions which made certain neighborhoods a problem to the metropolis drove out the churches; in fact, the churches seemed trapped by the forces of blight at work in the metropolis. The writer was led by the problems raised in these consultations to an evaluation of Protestant religious development in metropolitan areas. This book is the result of a search for answers to such questions as: How did we arrive at the present situation? What can we conclude about the religious revival on the basis of its effects on the metropolis? How can religious institutions become more responsible within metropolitan life?

Available studies of Protestantism provided material for this evaluation. Where data was incomplete, new areas of research were suggested. On the whole, however, the evidence was adequate to suggest the broad lines of a Protestant mission to the metropolis.

The problems of the Roman Catholic communion are neglected here because representative studies of their churches have yet to be made. Nevertheless, a strategy for Protestantism in the metropolis has considerable bearing on the course of Roman Catholic development, since the problem of a human environment in the metropolis imposes responsibilities upon all religious bodies.

Two words are used in a general way throughout this study—"Church" and "Protestant." The word "Church" (or church) has a great many meanings. A serious attempt has been made to use this word in contexts which make clear what is intended. When Church is capitalized it means the living manifestation in the world of the testimony of the Spirit to the Son. In this sense, historical embodiments of the Church are partial expressions, and occasionally denials, of the Church, and yet their partiality or disobedience is the vehicle whereby the Spirit proclaims God's life with man. Even the most disobedient communions are here called churches because they participate in the Church. The word "Protestant" is somewhat less ambiguous since it is used here largely in contrast to the Roman Catholic communion. There are considerable differences among the Protestant denominations or communions. For certain purposes these differences will be noted and even discussed in detail. Broadly speaking, Protestantism will refer to those communions which do not vest absolute power in the priestly hierarchy and, therefore, face somewhat different problems in their metropolitan mission.

A word of gratitude to the Frontier Evangelism Associates, who met under Parishfield auspices, expresses inadequately the writer's debt to them. The writer is especially grateful to Mel Ravitz, Paul Van Buren, Robert De Witt, John Walker, Emeric Kurtagh, David Kallen, Robert Scott, and Francis Ayres. Any study about the Church in society must draw upon the thought and research of many others whose contributions can only be partially recognized in the references. The footnotes are primarily intended to make such acknowledgments, but may also serve the special interest of those who wish to explore particular problems in more detail.

Gibson Winter

Chicago Divinity School
University of Chicago

The Suburban Captivity of the Churches

ONE

The Dilemma of Metropolitan Protestantism

The metropolis will be the principal field of Christian mission in the immediate future. This fact is generally acknowledged; however, the adequacy of the churches to this task is seldom discussed. The churches have had notable successes in the growing suburbs; they have suffered dismal failures in the central areas of the metropolis. No adequate explanation for this fact has been forthcoming, and yet the mission to the metropolis depends upon a ministry to the central city as well as the suburbs.

The metropolis now dominates the life and culture of the United States.[1] To be sure, the metropolis is a city, but it is a city with a difference, for it is the sphere of a massive agglomeration of people and the hub of an interdependent region of American society.[2] Religiousness or irreligiousness in the United States will depend upon the development of ministries in the metropolitan areas. This is where the masses of the population of the United States will work out their destinies in the coming generation; this is where the destiny of the nation will be decided for better or worse. Even a brief glance at metropolitan development confirms its pivotal place in American life.

THE GROWTH OF THE METROPOLIS

The notion of an *exploding* metropolis is a bit misleading. The metropolis is different from a city, but it evolves like a city. It would be difficult to say when the United States became urbanized, much less metropolitan. In 1790, 5 out of 100 people in the United States lived in urban areas; the era of the Founding Fathers was distinctly a rural period in American life, although cities were emerging and some of them were extremely influential. By the end of the Civil War, 25 out of 100 citizens were urbanites and cities were becoming increasingly significant in American life; immigration had already begun and industrialization was attracting workers to urban centers; nevertheless, the era of the city was in its infancy.[3] It was not until the end of World War I that one half the population of the United States was classified as urban; by 1950, 64 per cent of the population lived in urban areas. The American scene became dominantly urban at the turn of the century: the literary imagination had drawn many of its motifs from the urban scene in the latter part of the nineteenth century, but the shift from the frontier climate is most marked with the opening of the twentieth century; from this time forward the rural mind and agricultural occupations took second place in the life and thought of the American people. Agricultural life is still, of course, an important aspect of America, but rural patterns of thought are increasingly shaped by an urban climate. The city is now *the* milieu of American life.

In the course of urbanization, certain major centers of population emerged. Technically, these centers of population are called Standard Metropolitan Areas; they will be referred to here as metropolitan areas. (The technical definition of such centers includes a central city of 50,000 population or more, and contiguous areas of dense population which are integrated with the central city.)[4] By the turn of the century, 52 cities ranked as metropolitan areas; in other words, the major city had emerged by the close of the nineteenth century; fifty years later, there were 162 metropolitan areas in the United States. The trebling of major cities in this fifty-year period gives some indication of the increasing tendency of the American population to crowd into metropolitan centers. The actual density of population in these metropolitan areas is even more remarkable: in 1900, almost one out of three Americans lived in a metropolitan area; by 1950, almost two out of three. Present projections indicate that over two thirds of the population will reside in metropolitan areas by 1975. In brief, *the United States is now a metropolitan society*.

This picture of the evolving metropolis, however, fails to convey the full significance of the metropolis in the United States. The metropolis dominates a region of many states because it is the integrating center of services, communications, retailing activities, and production. Such centers play a strategic role in the organization of American life.[5] Sheer size is probably the best single measure of regional domination. Consider the fourteen largest metropolitan areas, each with at least a million in population; more than one half of the total metropolitan population live in one of these fourteen major metropolitan areas. As Amos Hawley has expressed it, "The United States population is living, to an increasing extent, in community aggregates of unprecedented size."[6]

Concentration of population is one index of metropolitan domination in American life, but it is not the key to the role of the metropolis. The metropolitan center is the heart of a network of communication which links suburbia, exurbia, and the hinterland to the metropolis. This network is partly fabricated by the spread of mass media of communication: the newspapers of the metropolis circulate throughout whole regions; the same is true of radio broadcasting and television programming. Transportation networks move people and goods to and from the metropolis; production and marketing are woven together in the metropolitan web; the specializations of an interdependent society are knit together through the activities of the metropolitan center. The metropolis is more than an area of high population density; metropolitan centers represent the multiple hearts of American social and economic organization.

The metropolis also shapes cultural styles and moral patterns, for domination of mass media gives the metropolis a strategic role in political, social, and cultural life. An obvious example is the effect of metropolitan clothing styles on the formerly isolated rural areas. Where mail-order houses used to offer rural styles in clothing, they now advertise a distinctly urban style. It would be difficult to think of a single facet of American culture not shaped in whole or part by the mental climate of the metropolis.

The metropolis is not static; it is a changing, dynamic process. This fact is most evident when one considers that metropolitan residents have been moving out from central cities to the suburbs for several generations; in fact, since 1920 the preponderant growth of metropolitan areas has been on the periphery of the central city.

This "satellite area" is actually a series of rings of decreasing population density. Large metropolitan areas are now composed of residential rings and satellite communities. The general pattern, familiar to most Americans, resembles a sprawl more than a community, but it is a sprawl unified by its relation to the heart of the metropolis.

The decentralization of metropolitan population follows a distinct pattern: moving outward from the heart of the central city to the rural hinterland, one finds progressively more expensive housing, more education, and higher incomes; as one approaches the center of the metropolis, the residents are increasingly unskilled, their incomes lower, their dwellings poorer.[7] There are, of course, variations in this pattern. As Harvey Zorbaugh indicated in the title of his classic study, *The Gold Coast and the Slum*, rich and poor districts do adjoin in certain areas of the central city; moreover, satellite communities are sometimes populated by industrial workers. It would be misleading to oversimplify the pattern of urban residence, but the distribution of metropolitan residence corresponds generally to the social and economic standing of the population. The spatial distances between people mirror the social and economic distance between them.

The residential pattern of the metropolis has emerged slowly: immigrations of foreign-born and in-migrations of rural workers have steadily replenished the population of the central cities; in reaction to these in-migrations, former residents moved toward the periphery as soon as they were financially able to do so; many could not change their residence, however, and have continued to live in the central city with the newcomers. The central city has been the scene of moving and shifting populations. The residential rings have also experienced change and movement, but their populations have been somewhat more stable.

An important change in the character of metropolitan populations occurred after World War I. Immigrants had been replenishing the work force in central cities for almost a century. With World War I immigration dropped to a trickle and was never revived in its previous form. After 1920, rural Whites and Negroes became a principal source of growth for metropolitan populations; in fact, this burden has fallen increasingly to rural Negroes and Puerto Ricans since that time.[8] Decentralization of the White population and increasing in-migration of Negroes have shaped the population distribution of many metropolitan areas since 1920.

If Negroes had been able to follow the pattern of social and economic upgrading which the foreign-born experienced, Negroes would now be distributed over the whole spectrum of residential areas. Two forces worked against the upgrading of Negroes in the metropolis: the job ceiling prevented Negroes from getting better jobs in urban areas, for job ceilings confined them to unskilled labor or service jobs—the only exceptions were those Negroes who gained higher positions by serving the Negro community in some business or professional capacity; the second force was residential segregation, for Negroes, poor and rich alike, were segregated within ghettos in the central city; year after year the density of Negro population within this limited space mounted; restrictive covenants against sale of homes to Negroes supported the wall of segregation; Negro in-migration was not checked, but Negro residential space remained constant.[9] When restrictive covenants were declared illegal by the Supreme Court in 1948, the Negroes began to move out of the ghettos, but informal covenants have confined them to the central cities. The net effect of this pattern in many metropolitan areas has been a growing domination of certain areas of central cities by Negroes.

Residential patterns in the metropolis are still changing. It is extremely difficult to generalize about these residential arrangements; nevertheless, one broad trend is emerging in many major metropolitan areas; working-class and lower middle-class people are concentrated in the central cities; middle- and upper-class Whites are moving rapidly to the satellite areas. The working-class and lower middle-class areas are becoming increasingly Negro in racial character; the central city, as administrative and political heart of the metropolis, is becoming a Negro community. This pattern is not fully developed, but it seems to be the shape of things to come. Morton Grodzins has described this racial schism within metropolitan populations in his monograph, *The Metropolitan Area as a Racial Problem*.[10] Grodzins estimates that in 1950 less than 5 per cent of urban Negroes were living in suburbs. At present, the racial schism is only partially developed. However, within thirty years Negroes will probably constitute from 25 to 50 per cent of the population of the centers of the metropolitan areas. This concentration of Negroes in central city areas consititutes, in brief, the most significant fact about distribution of peoples in the metropolis. Morton Grodzins sums up the situation as follows:

The larger evidence is neither that of social integration nor of intracommunity social gains. Rather it is evidence pointing to the expansion of Negro slums within the largest cities and the separation of Whites and Negroes by intracity neighborhoods, and especially on central city-suburban lines.[11]

The emerging racial schism is symptomatic of a much deeper strain within metropolitan life: this deeper tension is manifest in the separation of social classes; blue-collar and white-collar people are more and more separated; White Protestants are concentrated in middle- and upper-class areas and insulated from Negro Protestants. The Negro-White schism is the most serious but not the only form of the metropolitan schism. These considerations, however, turn our attention from the growth of the metropolis to its organization.

SOCIAL ORGANIZATION IN THE METROPOLIS

Two fundamental principles of social organization have cooperated and clashed in the birth of the metropolis. One principle is *interdependence*: industries, activities, jobs, and services are woven together into a complex web of interdependence; this web makes possible the emergence of the metropolis; the distinctive feature of such interdependence, moreover, is its impersonality. One does not ask who the person is but what he can do. One does not consider the family background of the owners of the manufacturing company but whether their products will meet the needs of a particular activity. The other major principle of social organization is

communal insulation: in contrast to the impersonal web of interdependence, a pattern of segregated communities of personal association shapes the neighborhoods of the metropolis; skin color,
style of life, manners, and even religious ties create autonomous
ghettos of people from a similar occupational level and ethnic background. In their personal communities, metropolitan people organize along exclusive lines; the impersonal interdependence of activities and services is balanced and sometimes contradicted by the
insulation of local neighborhoods.

The web of impersonal interdependence is the dominant motif
of the metropolis. Satellite and hinterland cities are interwoven
with the metropolis through innumerable interdependent activities
and services.[12] Most of us experience the interdependence of urban
life in a daily exchange of services; transactions with the clerk in
the store, the cashier at the counter, the usher at the theater. Buy-
ers, sellers, agencies, companies, manufacturing units, banks, stores,
and sundry other units of metropolitan life are interlaced in a web
of impersonal exchange and interdependence.

There are many kinds of interdependence in a metropolis: the
interdependence of outlying retail stores with central merchandis-
ing agencies is one kind; the interdependence of specialized
operations within a large manufacturing plant is another; the interdependence of community areas through common services of police, fire, and sanitation departments is another. These are the most
impersonal levels of interdependence within the metropolis. Exchange of money and goods at the local grocery exemplifies a more
personal level of interdependence; customers may know the local
grocer by name, exchange remarks about the weather, baseball, or
family life. Impersonality, however, is the usual mark of urban interdependence—few customers know the cashier in the supermar-
ket or the clerk in the department store; conversation usually
involves requests for information, wrapping, payment, and a mutual
thank you. Urban interdependence, even in human exchanges, is
normally very impersonal.

The impersonality of metropolitan interdependence is essential
to the extensive development of urban exchanges: if store clerks

were constantly bombarded with requests for personal loans, retailing would become too inefficient to continue; people of diverse cultures, races, and social classes can exchange goods and services effectively so long as they do not have to become personally involved with one another; they can work together in offices and factories so long as they do not feel personally responsible for one another. *Impersonality* in work and exchange is taken for granted in contemporary society; on this scale, however, it is a new phenomenon in human history. The extensive development of metropolitan life depends principally upon impersonal interdependence; it is this fact which makes interdependence dominant in the metropolis.[13]

There are many other aspects of interdependence in metropolitan life; the most important is the change in human communities which comes about with the expansion of interdependence. For example, if a man performs well in business or industry, he may be promoted to a position with a better income; in time, he will be able to buy a home in a better residential area; he and his family may lack the social background for this new neighborhood, but, barring certain restrictive covenants, they will be permitted to live there. If hiring were confined only to persons of a particular religious, racial, and national background, expansion of industry and services would be impossible. Expanding interdependence means broadening the base of employment and rewards; for example, American self-consciousness about the Negro question emerged when Negroes were needed in World War II for increased production and military service; it was quite evident, at this time, that expansion of interdependent activities was possible only if opportunities were extended to Negroes. A Negro could shoulder a gun or operate a machine as well as a White if he had opportunity and training; his race became irrelevant in the national crisis. Metropolitan life has expanded through a similar kind of impersonal evaluation of people on the basis of their potential contributions. This process breaks down the personal barriers which exclude persons; *who they are* becomes secondary to *what they can do*. When this question is asked, men of any color can rise.

In addition to opportunities for advancement, people need stable patterns of association; they need to be more than the impersonal functions they perform. They need to be evaluated for *who they are* as well as *what they can do*; they have to *be* as well as *do*. These deep needs for stability, recognition, and familiarity in personal associations lead to desires for continuing neighborhood relationships; in fact, they lead to a struggle for homogeneous neighborhoods. The interdependent activities of metropolitan life throw together Puerto Ricans, Negroes, blue collar, white collar, old residents, and newcomers. Residential neighborhoods, however, strive to preserve enclaves of people of similar racial, national, religious, and social-class character—all Jewish, or all middle class, or all White. The residential community strives for stability by insulating itself against contacts with social differences which the interdependent metropolis overlooks. The physical pattern of residential areas in the metropolis mirrors the social distances between people because neighborhood is based on similarity in social and economic position; the market place of the metropolis, by contrast, embraces the whole spectrum of social and economic differences. Blue collar and white collar share the street and separate by neighborhoods. The open market and the insulated neighborhood represent the two types of metropolitan organization—impersonal interdependence and insulated, communal solidarity, inclusiveness and exclusiveness, common humanity and social differences.

Association by likeness is the principle of neighborhood life. It may take one of several forms. Louis Wirth's analysis of *The Ghetto* is a classic in the interpretation of this principle of insulated community.[14] Although the term "ghetto" originally referred to the excluded Jewish community, there are ethnic, racial, and social-class ghettos in the metropolis. Insulated residential community on the basis of likeness has provided a new kind of ghetto as the pattern of stability for the social, economic, racial, and religious strata of the metropolis; neighborhood comes to mean an island of homogeneous people.

In one of his essays, Louis Wirth defined a city as "a relatively large, dense, and permanent settlement of socially heterogeneous individuals."[15] This definition stresses the agglomeration of metropolitan people; it emphasizes the principal effect of impersonal interdependence. This heterogeneity to which he referred, however, is actually played down in the normal exchanges of metropolitan life; interchanges in the market are kept on an impersonal and limited basis; in their exchanges with one another, metropolitan people minimize differences by not becoming personally involved. This states the case too extremely, but it suggests the kind of relationship in which social differences are minimized for the sake of getting along and doing business. Working together in a shop creates an opportunity for personal relationships, but personal association is not the main reason for being in the shop. The opposite is true in the neighborhood: the residential life of the metropolis presents an aggregate of homogeneous groupings, a mosaic of residential communities grouped according to social, racial, and economic similarities.

Whites in the metropolis have associated residentially largely on the basis of social and economic rank; their differences have been principally those of culture, education, style of life, and occupational level. The spread of metropolitan population from inner city to satellite areas mirrors these economic and social differences in the White population. To be sure, residential mobility and social climbing in the metropolis create constant change in the complexion of metropolitan communities; nevertheless, incoming residents will tend to be similar in social and economic rank to resident members of the community. Where choice can be exercised, communities of similar social class, ethnic, racial, and even religious complexion emerge. These communities are insulated against outsiders. They strive to preserve a community of likeness against the disruptive forces of metropolitan growth.

Personal association is confined largely to residential and familial communities within the metropolis. Market, shop, office, store, and factory are spheres of impersonal dealings and manipulations; but a person's social identity—who he is in the human community of persons, *as a person*—is rooted primarily in the residential sphere of personal association. One's sense of continuity, stability, and order is created primarily through the responses of family and, possibly, neighborhood. These are the primary ties that form the basis for personal and social identity in human life; when men and women cannot find a place within a personal community of identity, their lives become disoriented and even destructive. A familiar form of such breakdown in the metropolis is the delinquent.

Association by likeness helps to create a community of identity in a changing metropolis, because persons feel safe when they can predict the responses of those with whom they associate. By contrast, it makes little difference to a foreman whether or not his subordinate responds warmly to him; he may worry about it, but he can tolerate dislike so long as it does not slow down the work. The same foreman, however, will feel quite differently about the responses of his wife and children; his family is a crucial community of social identity; if he lives in a fairly stable neighborhood, he will also be concerned about the attitudes of his neighbors or friends toward him; he wants to be wanted in his communities of identity. Most people are concerned about the responses they arouse within their sphere of personal associations; differences of race, nationality, religion, style of life, and social rank seem to threaten the harmony of such communities; it is this threat which makes residential communities so sensitive to the intrusion of outsiders. The residential community is the one sphere of metropolitan life where people feel free to choose their associates; the newcomer of different race or nationality might prove to be an excellent neighbor; the point, however, is not whether the newcomer might be a good neighbor but rather that he is perceived as a threat to the harmony of the homogeneous, residential area.

Urban life from earliest times has been a conglomeration of local enclaves built around occupational, ethnic, religious, racial, or other interests. This phenomenon is not new in urban areas; several new factors, however, have exacerbated the struggle for homogeneous neighborhoods and altered the significance of these enclaves for the churches.

The Back of the Yards Council in Chicago illustrates the kinds of changes which make the struggle for an insulated neighborhood a new kind of problem for the metropolis and the churches. Saul Alinsky made the Back of the Yards familiar by his discussion of its development in his book, *Reveille for Radicals*. This residential area centered around the meat-packing industry. The area had been very disorganized as a consequence of the instability of the industry, the rapid movement of people in and out of the area, and the lack of political self-consciousness of the residents; nevertheless, common occupational, religious, ethnic, and political interests made it possible to develop a significant communal organization in the area. The Back of the Yards became what many political wards of the larger urban areas had been throughout the latter part of the nineteenth century and even up to the 1920s; it became a politically self-conscious area with sufficient economic, ethnic, religious, and racial similarity to provide a stable community of identity for the residents. The Back of the Yards Council was, in this sense, an attempt to re-create some of the stabilizing features of the "natural" economic, ethnic, and religious communities which made the older American city a mosaic of national and political groups.

At the time that Saul Alinsky and his organization were attempting to create a common life in the Back of the Yards, the forces of metropolitan development had already dissolved many of the solidarities in the community around the stockyards: the second- and third-generation ethnics no longer felt so strongly the ties of national origin; the Negro community was expanding on the edges of the area; political unity had been undermined by rapid residential mobility; only religious ties and certain economic interests could be used to mobilize the political unity of the area.[16] However, residential community is now undergoing even more serious disruption in the course of metropolitan development. Rapid transportation has made it possible to decentralize industry to less expensive properties, so that place of employment and area of residence are more and more segregated. The Back of the Yards Council is experiencing this new stage in metropolitan development in the removal of slaughtering and packing from the stockyards area in Chicago—the very name of the community organization may be an anachronism within a decade. Moreover, racial differences have become a pressing problem to homogeneous communities, since Negroes are slowly gaining the right to employment and will soon begin to climb the social and economic ladders. The threads of common life upon which the Back of the Yards Council was built—common occupation, ethnic and racial similarity—are disappearing. The remaining threads of common life are social class (blue collar or white collar), race, and, to some degree, religion.

Attempts to preserve stable neighborhoods have now become a struggle to maintain a color line along with homogeneity of class. Religious affiliation (along the tripartite lines of Catholic, Protestant, or Jew, in Will Herberg's phraseology) has also been drawn into this struggle. In general, the organic (or "natural") solidarity which created the ethnic and political mosaic of American cities in the nineteenth century is dissolving; a panic to preserve social, economic, and racial similarities in residential areas has developed around this void in local community. The net effect of this panic in residential areas—a panic engendered and aggravated by the rapidity of social changes in the metropolis—has been the alignment of religious associations with the struggle for homogeneous and racially segregated neighborhoods. The familiar cliché that eleven o'clock on Sunday morning is the most segregated hour in the United States points up this unholy alliance of religious and racial segregation, an alliance whose real purpose is to preserve insulated, residential communities. To understand this development is not to excuse the unholy alliance, but it does provide some basis for discussing the real issue confronting metropolitan churches. The racial schism of the metropolis is a symptom of the desperate struggle for stable communal areas—a struggle which has become pathological, for it is an attempt to insulate neighborhood areas against outsiders, to set the clock back a hundred years. At present, this struggle impinges sharply on the Negro community, for the struggle takes the form of residential segregation and discrimination. The solution of the Negro problem, however, will leave the metropolis with its basic difficulty unresolved, for impersonal interdependence generates constant change, transforming town to city, city to metropolis, metropolitan area to strip city, and undermining every local community. The metropolis is inclusive. Churches that identify with local areas become exclusive and antimetropolitan.

The conflict between expanding interdependence and attempts to stabilize residential communities by insulating them against outsiders provides the milieu of the Church's mission in the city. The net effect of the conflict between cosmopolitan expansion and local cohesiveness has been a breakdown in communication in the metropolis: local communities have ceased to operate as significant centers of political interest, for their local identity is based on shallow class conformity; collective control of political life has been seized by élite groups; community of interest has dissolved in residential areas, so that local communities are swept away overnight with rumors of racial change (a White area can be "bombed" by hiring real estate speculators to walk through the area). Attempts at urban renewal and redevelopment have become highly localized ventures, so that improvement in one area simply dislocates large populations of underprivileged people who overcrowd an adjoining area. In general, the metropolis is being transformed from a mosaic of ethnic and political communities into a warring struggle of each neighborhood against all—a struggle for survival in which every community, whether inside or outside the central city, knows that blight will reach it within two decades if it is not already at the door.

This breakdown of communication, and consequently of corporate government, creates a void which is filled with the arbitrary action of a political élite who must act and yet cannot act responsibly. Local centers of political interest and concern—the middle levels of power—which are assumed as the operating base of a democracy are destroyed. Meanwhile, community breaks down at both local and metropolitan levels. People act to preserve the local residential community, but in doing so violate the communal interests of the metropolitan area; for example, they exclude Negroes and force overcrowding in other areas, or they try to preserve independence from metropolitan government and force up costs of government and services in their own locality and in the central city. It is a war of each against all. Impersonal interdependence has made possible a rapid expansion of the size and productivity of the metropolis, but it has also disrupted local communities to such an extent that the metropolitan area has become an arena of struggle for the preservation of local enclaves—a desperate clutching for some straw of similarity on which to build a racial or religious community of identity. The more tenuous the common bond, the more tenaciously it is clutched. The status panic which has caught the public interest in recent years is likewise a symptom of this deeper struggle for a community of identity through the insulation of groups of a similar social and economic level. The two principles of social organization in the metropolis—impersonal interdependence and segregation by community of identity—are now polarized, and the destructive effects are being felt in spreading juvenile delinquency, crime, social disorganization, the vicious circle of urban blight, and deepening racial schism. The struggle for stable neighborhoods has made segregation along racial and/or class lines endemic to the metropolis.

The problem of the churches in the metropolis is intimately bound up with this conflict between the major principles of social organization in metropolitan life; in fact, the mission of the Church in the metropolis can only be understood in the light of this polarization of the principles of metropolitan organization. Since churches have traditionally anchored their communal life in residential areas, they inevitably become victims of the pathology that assails neighborhood life, whether it be small-town gossip or metropolitan discrimination. The revival of religious interest and the peculiar pattern of religious development in the metropolis are interwoven with the special problems attendant upon the struggle to stabilize local communities. These problems create the peculiar dilemma confronting Protestantism in the metropolis. How can an inclusive message be mediated through an exclusive group, when the principle of exclusiveness is social-class identity rather than a gift of faith which is open to all?

THE DILEMMA OF METROPOLITAN PROTESTANTISM

The major denominations of Protestantism are gradually becoming metropolitan in character; nevertheless, Protestant memberships are still more rural than would be expected in view of the growing concentration of people in the metropolis. A report for 1953 indicated that only 46 per cent of Protestant strength was in metropolitan areas, although 56 per cent of the total population resided in these areas at the time.[17] In view of the traditionally rural character of Protestantism, this is a reasonable showing. Certain denominations are, of course, markedly urban, whereas several large denominations continue to be primarily rural. In general, the churches have prospered in the course of urbanization, and are still growing.

A brief indication of recent religious growth may suggest the mental climate that pervades the churches. In the 1958 yearbook, contributions to most of the major bodies showed a gain of 11 per cent over the preceding year.[18] Despite inflation, this is a notable gain. Church membership was 62 per cent of total population in 1956 as compared to 49 per cent in 1940. Opinion polls of attendance at church by adults indicated that 41 per cent of the respondents attended in the week preceding the interview in 1939 as compared to 51 per cent in 1957. Construction of new church buildings reflects somewhat more closely the state of the economy; however, comparing the lush years of 1928 and 1956, expenditures on new building show roughly a 400 per cent increase by 1956. These figures give some hint of the increase in religious interest.

The metropolitan problem of the churches is not a failure in organizational growth; the present rate of metropolitan expansion among the churches should soon bring their religious constituencies into line with general population trends. Metropolitan churches are confronted with a dilemma between organizational expansion and responsibility for the central city—at least, this is the superficial way in which the problem emerges. Satellite areas, as indicated above, are growing rapidly; the churches are capitalizing on this growth with an unprecedented expansion; simultaneously, however, the churches are losing contact with the central city areas —at least, this is true of the major denominations of White Protestantism. The metropolitan schism is present within the life of Protestantism: Negro and sectarian churches are multiplying in the central cities, but they are not in a position to come to grips with the social disorganization of the central city areas; for the most part they are small, inadequately staffed churches; ethnic churches are losing their ethnic traditions and their constituencies are moving to middle-class areas; the major White denominations are concentrated on the periphery of the city; the central city churches of these denominations recruit more than 50 per cent of their memberships from a great distance; these central city churches, meanwhile, lose members while satellite churches grow. Protestantism divides along racial lines and between blue-collar and white-collar populations. The major denominations, whose membership includes from 80 to 90 per cent of all Protestants, are being alienated from the peoples and problems of the central cities; the White branches of the major denominations are aligned with the middle-class, suburban side of the social-class and racial schism.

The schism in Protestantism is also reflected in the mixed attitudes of religious leaders toward metropolitan needs. Denominational leaders have watched the new residential areas surrounding the central cities with greedy eyes. These are largely middle- and upper-class residential areas; they have adequate resources for constructing church buildings; their residents are responsive to religious programs; in fact, denominational leaders call these "high potential areas,"—and they do not mean potential for prayer. In recent decades almost exclusive attention has been given to establishing churches in suburban areas. Denominations have joined forces for the development of new churches through federations and councils of churches; they have set up planning staffs for co-operative church extension, usually called comity.[19] Although comity programs for church extension vary considerably, all of them attempt to allocate new residential areas to different denominations in order to avoid duplication in expenditure and prevent over-churching of particular areas. Comity, to use a phrase from H. Paul Douglass, is a combination of ecclesiastical eugenics and planned parenthood. The growing co-operation on comity is an index of the extent to which organizational growth has been central to denominational concerns: the satellite areas have increased the demand for churches; denominational co-operation has attended to this demand.

Concentration on satellite areas is perfectly understandable in terms of the organizational interests of the denominations; central city areas, particularly the inner zones of the central city, confront the churches with innumerable problems; in fact, congregations have been retreating from these areas for decades, and only a few churches have been able to remain active in these parts of the cities. The central city is littered with decaying church buildings in areas of rapid population change. It has been difficult to obtain pastors for these churches; in fact, change of pastorate is almost an annual phenomenon. In recent years, however, the denominations have become aware that they were losing touch with central city areas, and that greed for growth was driving them to the outer zones of the central city. Programs of church extension have strengthened the major denominations in the satellite areas, but at the risk of losing touch with the heart of the metropolis. Policies of church extension, therefore, are arousing the anxieties of some farsighted denominational leaders: on the one hand, they are committed to a policy of extension on the growing perimeter of the cities; on the other, they sense that this policy is disengaging the churches from the center of the metropolis; since the whole central city is deteriorating rapidly, the net effect is to alienate the churches from the central cities.

Denominational leaders are troubled with problems even more serious than the schism between the central city and satellite areas. The preceding discussion has focused on this schism in the ministry to the city, but the alienation from metropolitan life runs much deeper, for the identification of congregational life with neighborhoods also means insulation from metropolitan concerns. At a meeting of City Churchmen of the United Church of Christ in 1958, John Osman said ,"Religion today is challenged to create an urban civilization. . . . Religion has abandoned the city and left its redemption to business and industry. . . . Only religion can regenerate our cities by making them a place for spiritual growth."[20] At the same meeting, Truman B. Douglass said, "Not only has American Protestantism failed to penetrate the culture of modern cities, it has largely refused to take that culture seriously, and it has withdrawn from the task of relating the Christian faith to the problems and needs of human beings in contemporary urban society."[21] These statements reflect a profound concern with the alienation of the churches from urban culture—the religious betrayal of the metropolis—and express the views of a prophetic minority in the churches.

The tension between the churches' responsibility for metropolitan life and their desire for suburban growth revealed itself at a meeting of Methodist leaders in 1959. John Wicklein of the New York *Times* headlined his report of the meeting with this statement: "The Methodist Church, the largest Protestant denomination in the country, is dying out in the cities."[22] His report also contains an observation made at this meeting by a Methodist leader: "In Boston five churches died in ten years, leaving only five surviving in the inner city."[23]

At this Methodist meeting, concern focused on the schism between central city and satellite areas; disengagement of Protestant churches from the central city is the most obvious and manifest form of alienation from metropolitan life, since the heart of the metropolis continues to be a significant center of population, a pivot of political power. The central city is the area which suffers most radically from the disorganizing effects of urban life; it is the area of most pressing personal and social need and the scene of repeated defeats for the churches. Every venture in the inner city involves exorbitant cost in personnel and money, with little hope of return in new members or funds. Every advance toward the satellite areas, on the other hand, promises unlimited return with minimal outlay. The organizational extension of Protestantism has followed the line of least resistance; church extension, thus, runs counter to the metropolitan responsibility of Protestantism, since it threatens to alienate the major White denominations from the central city areas. Denominations cannot continue their organizational growth without sacrificing their moral and religious responsibility to the total metropolitan area or to about one half of the metropolitan population. This is the dilemma which has faced Protestantism; its roots, however, lie deeper than the mistaken strategy of denominational leaders.

The metropolis has become an interdependent whole without adequate internal processes of communication to provide stability and direction. The most obvious symptom of this internal breakdown is the lack of political coherence in the metropolitan area—a void which has the most serious consequences for every aspect of metropolitan life, from park planning to police protection. The problem of the churches is that their strength centers in the fabric of a local community, for both parochial and congregational forms of religious organization emerged as expressions of cohesive, local communities in the villages of feudal Europe and in the local enclaves of medieval cities. When metropolitan changes practically dissolved neighborhood communities, the churches were left without any communal fabric to sustain their congregational life. Meanwhile, the breakdown of communication in the metropolitan area had created a search for insulated neighborhoods; hence, the neighborhoods in which the churches vested their basic unit of organization—parish or congregation—became the scene of a struggle for insulation. Segregation became the path to stability. While the metropolis needed new channels of communication, the more homogeneous communities on the fringe of the city were struggling to break communication with other groups in the metropolis. These citadels became dungeons for congregational and parochial life. The churches entered a period of suburban captivity, deserted the central city and aligned themselves with the status panic, becoming mere refuges for the fleeing middle classes. The churches, which should have facilitated communication, became instruments to block it.

The exodus from the central city reveals the struggle of middle-class people to fabricate some semblance of common life through a religious congregation. This struggle is a tragic story in the history of the Christian ministry to the metropolis, since it led to the unchurching of blue-collar people and the provision of ministry almost exclusively on the basis of power to pay—a ministry which was becoming increasingly costly in training and paraphernalia. The struggle for stability led to an uprooting of the congregations, since the emerging middle classes, which carried the weight of the Protestant population, were moving nearer and nearer to the edge of the city. The very dependence of congregational and parochial life upon a fabric of cohesive community made them vulnerable to the suburban captivity, for here at least they could find some semblance of common life to sustain their rituals. Nevertheless, the relationship of the major denominations to the middle classes was a two-way street, for the middle classes used the congregation as a platform upon which to build a sense of belonging and tradition, even as the major denominations used the middle classes as a pool for recruitment. In this way the exodus from the central city and the concentration on suburban growth were both products of the peculiar needs of the middle classes and the particular vulnerability of the major denominations in the changing metropolis.

The activity of the congregations of the major denominations and their appalling superficiality have often been noted by foreign observers; these visitors from afar look wistfully at church activities and budgets but stand aghast before the spiritual emptiness of these associations. This strange combination of vitality and emptiness can be understood in the light of the peculiar coalition between the major denominations and the emerging middle class. A wholly new style of religious life emerged in this coalition; in fact, the constellation of forces at work in the metropolis gave birth to the organization church. The bond between the organization church and the particular interests and needs of the white-collar ranks can be discerned, but the real problem remains as to whether this fabricated community can serve as a platform for a mission to the metropolis or must be abandoned for a renewed church.

The breakdown of local community meant the dissolution of the fabric which had made sense of congregational life, for without this communal fabric the congregation met in a vacuum, no longer a fellowship representing the community from which it was called. Assembled from no real community and witnessing to none, it merely contemplated its own budget. The same thing happened to the parish, for the parochial form had represented a geographical area in which economic, political, and communal interests intersected. When the residential area became a place for social and economic insulation, the parish became a highly segregated community which could barely survive the rapid population changes to which most metropolitan neighborhoods were subject. In either case, the breakdown of local community gave rise to an organization church as a substitute form of community. The principal difficulty lay in the fact that the organization church was neither a community of faith nor a truly universal form of organization which could bring together the conflicting and estranged elements in the metropolis, for the organization was anchored in a segregated context rather than a ministry. The organization church can be a platform for a mission and an appropriate form for reconciling diverse elements in the metropolis only insofar as it can be freed from the shackles of local enclaves. This is the real problem confronting Protestantism in the metropolis. The solution of this problem can pave the way for the churches to renew their ministry to the metropolis and ultimately to reopen communication in the metropolitan area.

This verdict—the essentially optimistic view that major denominations have a working base from which to launch a mission to the whole metropolis and to halt their flight into middle-class enclaves—has some warrant in recent developments among the churches. On May 1, 1960, Protestants, Catholics, and Jews joined together for a Conference on Problems of Housing in the Chicago Metropolitan Area. It was an historic occasion both because these groups have had relatively little communication and because they joined forces in confronting one of the most difficult problems in a metropolitan area. This interfaith venture into metropolitan communication over crucial problems of metropolitan community may come to nothing, but it is at least a straw in the wind. The great religious faiths which have emerged on the American scene are powerful forces for communication and renewal when they begin to look toward human needs in contemporary life. They can be vehicles of reconciliation and communication, even as the organization churches can provide the base for a totally new form of

ministry to the metropolitan area. This is the promise of the
churches in the metropolis, though at the moment no more than
promise, since these same churches are largely preoccupied with
organizational interests.

The subsequent discussion devotes little attention to the problems of interfaith communication, and even scants the difficulties
of interdenominational union. Such omissions are justified in part
by the attention being given to these problems by other writers,
but more particularly by the importance of the central concern of
this evaluation—that is, the actual fabric of the religious community
in the metropolis and its potential for a mission to the metropolitan
area. Ultimately, the only important question about any congregation or religious group is this: in what ways is it an expression of
ministry in faith and obedience? The tragedy of the organization
church has been its substitution of survival for ministry. Its promise
lies in its resources for ministry in a mass society. The path to interfaith co-operation and interdenominational union will be found, as
the title of a book by Visser t'Hooft so well expresses it, under
The Pressure of Our Common Calling. This calling and our po-
tentiality for fulfilling it will occupy the center of the stage at every
point in this evaluation of the emergence of the organization
church. It is from the inner grace of those called to the ministry
that the organization church will find the strength to fulfill its role
as a mission rather than a refuge from the metropolitan struggle for
a human environment.

TWO: **The Exodus**

Protestantism was on the move from 1870 to 1950; the major denominations of White Protestantism were moving outward from central city areas to the suburbs during most of this period. This decentralization of Protestantism was a reaction to changes in metropolitan population; it was also evidence of the uprooting of the congregations from their neighborhoods; in fact, neighborhoods became places of residence instead of communities. The net effect of this outward movement has been a growing insulation of the major denominations from the people of the central cities.

The Protestant exodus from the central city was partly a consequence of the upgrading of native-born White Protestants. Upgrading here means movement upward in social rank from manual to nonmanual work.[1] Whatever one's ideas about the equality of all kinds of work, Americans accord higher prestige to nonmanual work. Although many skilled workers receive higher incomes than the lowest ranks of nonmanual workers, the white collar is invariably a sign of higher social rank.[2] Native-born urban Whites had many opportunities to move from manual to nonmanual work between 1870 and 1950; in fact, this upgrading had been going on since the great immigrations of the mid-nineteenth century.

Upgrading in a metropolitan area usually leads to residential movement away from the inner city. The growth of business and industrial establishments expand the area of the inner city; poorer populations are pushed toward the perimeter of this expanding center; working-class residential areas are invaded by the lowest ranks in the labor force; better residential areas feel the outward movement of the skilled ranks of the labor force; thus, outward movement and upgrading go hand in hand with urban expansion.[3] By 1920, population outside the central cities had begun to increase disproportionately; the suburban trickle had become a flood; movement from "dirty" work to "clean" work accelerated residential movement from the central city to the suburban fringe.[4]

White Protestants were in the vanguard of the suburban movement, being advantageously placed to benefit by the expansion in numbers of clean jobs. The outward tide of middle-class movement became simultaneously an exodus of White Protestantism.[5] Urban Protestantism became suburban Protestantism in less than a century. White Protestant outposts in central areas of the metropolis are today either heavily subsidized by nonresident congregations or struggling for survival against heavy odds. In the continuing metropolitan sprawl, Protestant churches are being established throughout the lower middle- and upper middle-class areas surrounding the central cities. Unless this tide is reversed, White Protestantism will have few remaining churches within the perimeter of the central cities by 1975; moreover, these remaining churches will be supported by upper-class groups in high-rent apartments or by clusters of middle-class people in selected areas of the city.[6] In the light of the broad population trend of recent decades, the suburbanization of Protestantism seems to be an inevitable consequence of the upgrading of native-born urban Whites.

The meaning of the upgrading of major denominations of White Protestantism is not very clear, since the old-line denominations were already identified with the middle classes in the latter part of the nineteenth century. Although no accurate studies of the social-class composition of these denominations are available, religious leaders often protested the alienation of Protestantism from the working classes at this time.[7] Many poorer areas of the major cities were stripped of churches in the latter part of the nineteenth century; in fact, Protestant congregations at this time were closely identified with the petty bourgeoisie and the upper classes; consequently, the notion of upgrading must be used with considerable caution.

The major denominations were upgraded in the course of the exodus from the central city by drawing their memberships more and more exclusively from people in nonmanual occupations; these denominations became increasingly identified with the middle class.

The reduced proportion of manual workers in the churches came about in several ways: native-born White urbanites were being upgraded during this period, so that a "natural" upward mobility occurred;[8] moreover, the removal of church sites to better residential locations meant the abandonment of many members who could not move from the former location; churches of major denominations were thus sloughing off their lower-class members and adding new members in districts of higher prestige.[9] Major denominations were upgraded, therefore, as they identified themselves more closely with the middle class. These denominations have always had manual workers in their membership, but from 1870 to 1950 the percentage of manual workers in major denominations was sharply reduced.

Another kind of upgrading also occurred among major denominations. Although denominational congregations were primarily middle class in the latter part of the nineteenth century, their buildings were located in the central city areas. The cleavage between old-line Protestantism and the working class was created by social rather than physical distance. The size and nature of cities at this time made this development inevitable. Furthermore, shorter physical distances created real physical barriers in a time when rapid transportation was only beginning to alter the pattern of metropolitan life. The suburbanization of the major White denominations has enormously increased the physical distance between the Protestant churches and working-class people. If and when working-class people begin to move to the suburbs, as they now do in central sections of satellite areas, some of these physical barriers may be overcome. However, it has become less and less meaningful to charge denominational congregations with their responsibilities to the working classes and the Negro population, since an increasing proportion of denominational congregations are insulated from these segments of the population by the line which separates suburbia from the central city. In this sense, the upgrading of the major White denominations also means physical insulation from manual workers; most Protestant congregations are now thoroughly divorced from the residential locales of working people.

The upgrading of White Protestant congregations has both internal and external aspects. Internal upgrading came about by sloughing off lower-class members who were not in a position to move toward the suburbs; external upgrading resulted from increasing the physical distance between denominational churches and working-class people. Upgrading continues today, since central city churches are rapidly losing ground while suburban churches are increasing their memberships.[10] Collapse of central city churches means abandoning large numbers of the congregation to an inadequate ministry, while suburban gains mean increased recruitment from the upper social ranks. The Protestant exodus is an index of selective Protestant growth among the upper social ranks; it is also an index of the disengagement of major denominations from the people and problems of the central city areas. Whatever the constituency of Protestantism may have been in the nineteenth century, it became increasingly middle class and physically more insulated from the working classes during the Protestant exodus.

Population changes were the precipitating factor in the Protestant exodus; many congregations changed the location of their churches every decade or two after 1850.[11] Industrial expansion brought waves of immigration; the more prosperous church members moved outward with each new wave; in many cases, the congregations sold their buildings and built new churches in the better residential areas; in fact, the expansion of major cities can be traced by mapping the location and relocation of Protestant congregations.[12] Particular immigrations and in-migrations had distinctive effects on the major denominations: they led uniformly to Protestant movement, but the implications for Protestantism were not always the same. The specific character of these effects can be seen by considering the actual population movements.

Protestantism reacted against several types of population movement between 1870 and 1950. The *Roman Catholic* immigrations were obviously a serious problem to the major denominations; concentrations of Roman Catholic immigrants made some residential areas untenable for Protestant congregations. When Roman Catholic concentration is combined with an expansion of commercial districts, a certain amount of Protestant movement is inevitable. Many church buildings were vacated during these great immigrations; more seriously, however, the Protestant retreat from largely Roman Catholic areas often meant the abandonment of minority groups of Protestants. In the early period of urban growth, the Protestant exodus meant stripping inner city areas of religious institutions, since Roman Catholic churches could not be established in sufficient numbers to meet the waves of immigration.[13]

Immigrations of *foreign-born Protestants* likewise confronted native-born Protestantism with serious problems; ethnic communities developed their own religious institutions, and foreign-born Protestants affiliated with them.[14] How much this tendency was aggravated by attitudes of native-born Whites would be hard to assess. It is clear, however, that local Protestants found foreign-born people strange and viewed them as aliens.[15] Some Protestant denominations developed foreign-language churches and missions for Protestant immigrants, but such congregations rarely mixed immigrants with the native-born.

St. Louis is an example of heavy Protestant immigration subsequently developing into separate streams of Protestantism. German-speaking Protestants developed their own institutions and followed a separate path of outward movement in the second generation.[16] Native-born Protestantism beat a retreat from the immigrant settlements, moving toward the residential areas of highest prestige. These movements meant a failure to solidify Protestant forces and a consequent abandonment of less mobile members of the native-born congregations.

In-migrations of *rural White Protestants* also confronted the major denominations with a problem; rural newcomers brought a different style of life, were confined largely to the lower rungs of the economic ladder, and were treated as aliens. Naturally, they gravitated to religious sects which fitted their own needs, as ethnics had attached themselves to ethnic communities. The Protestant retreat and the search by newcomers for a familiar style of religious observance contributed also to the alienation of rural Protestants from the major denominations. Since the sects were small groups and ministered to a fragment of the rural in-migration, the net effect of the exodus was to increase the unchurched populations of the central cities.[17] This problem continues to face the major denominations, since rural Whites are still pouring into the central cities. The significant fact about the retreat from rural newcomers is that these folk were traditionally Protestant.[18] The Protestant retreat, in this instance, meant a radical impoverishment of the ministry to these areas and unchurched large numbers of rural in-migrants. The derelict churches which remained could not provide adequate ministries for their own constituencies and lacked the vitality and interest to recruit substantially from the newcomer groups. These weakened churches provided vulnerable points for invasion by left-wing, fundamentalist groups.[19] Protestant gains in membership through movement to the best residential areas were counterbalanced by heavy losses in churches and memberships in the central areas of the city.

The pattern of *Negro in-migration* to metropolitan areas had somewhat different effects on the major denominations. Negroes entered urban areas with a Protestant tradition; nevertheless, they represented the most serious threat to White Protestantism of all the new population groups. Negroes had trickled into urban areas during the nineteenth century; there were small colonies of Negroes in the larger cities by the turn of the century; however, Negro in-migration increased rapidly during World War I, and after 1920 became a major source of metropolitan growth. In-migration of Negroes uniformly accelerated the withdrawal of White Protestantism; in fact, the two cultures were totally estranged.[20] Since World War II denominational leadership has taken a new tack and urged integration of Negroes into local White congregations, but this counsel requires a different kind of congregation to become more than a gesture.[21]

The retreat from the Negro occurred in a two-phase movement: higher-status congregations withdrew with the first threat of Negro invasion; middle- and lower middle-class congregations moved more slowly; consequently, the secondary withdrawal of Protestantism came about through attrition.[22] The lower-status congregations, in other words, suffered losses of membership for years before finally collapsing, holding consistently to the pattern of an all-White constituency.[23]

This two-phase retreat from the Protestant Negro indicates the special character of the Negro problem in the metropolitan area. Higher-status congregations moved every decade or so; the rumor of Negro movement was sufficient to prompt their exodus. The "tip-point" for higher-status congregations (meaning the point at which they perceive the area as Negro) occurred with the mere threat of Negro movement, rather than at the point of heavy Negro concentration. (Tip-point usually refers to that proportion of Negroes in a residential area which will cause most, if not all, Whites to leave—in other words, that point where an area swings to almost total Negro occupancy.) The tip-point for higher-status congregations corresponded roughly to the residential movement of their own constituencies prior to Negro movement, and was often preceded by movements of the Jewish community. Negroes did not occupy an entire neighborhood on first invading an area; consequently, many lower-status Whites continued to live there. Lower middle-class White congregations dwindled slowly as Negroes continued to increase in numbers in these areas; increases in the Negro population in Chicago from 1920 to 1940, for example, were not accompanied by significant increases in the residential space available to Negroes; the Negro population was simply crowded more densely into the available buildings within the Negro ghetto. The increase of Negro population meant a corresponding decrease in the number of Whites remaining in the area; the secondary tip-point for White Protestant churches seems to have been at roughly 40 per cent. When Negroes represented about two fifths of the residents of an area, all Protestant churches had moved or disbanded.[24] The retreat of higher-status Protestant churches at the first tip-point impoverished the Protestant ministry to the area; the secondary withdrawal at the 40 per cent tip-point caused the abandonment of the remaining White Protestant population.

The Supreme Court decision against restrictive covenants in 1948 accelerated residential movements of Negroes and closed the interval between the two tip-points. Today White Protestantism may disappear from a residential area in a matter of months. Very few higher-status congregations serve both Negroes and Whites; it is the middle-status congregations of the central city that bear the brunt of conflict at these points of racial intersection. Some of them have attempted to desegregate; few have been successful, however, since residential areas are almost totally Negro before such an integrated pattern can offset the withdrawal of Whites. The Negro movement and White retreat have led to the withdrawal of major denominations of White Protestantism from many areas of the central city.

To the extent that Negroes gravitated to their own churches in the course of urbanization, they followed the pattern of the foreign-born and the rural Whites. Negro churches have varied considerably in quality: some Negro churches have had ministries of the highest quality and have shown concern for their membership; in general, however, the Negro community has been overchurched with struggling congregations and inadequately trained ministries. In retrospect, it is easy to say that the major denominations of White Protestantism might have corrected this situation through a more positive attitude toward the Negro newcomer; actually, it is too late to alter the situation.[25] Negro Protestantism will have to build an adequate ministry and religious life under the most difficult circumstances, for the overcrowding of Negro residential areas has caused the spread of urban blight with each new movement of the Negro population.[26] Inner city blight is rapidly consuming the total area of the central city, and, although the stronger forces in Negro Protestantism have fought this blight and worked for better housing, the Negro churches are no more able to cope with this situation than the major denominations.[27] Every step toward an integrated church threatens the status of the Negro ministry; every attempt to build a strong congregation is undermined by the rapidly spreading blight. Encounters between White and Negro Protestantism still occur principally at the highest denominational levels, and most of these interchanges are superficial. The long tradition of social apartheid has eventuated in a schism of the first magnitude in metropolitan Protestantism.[28] The Protestant exodus brought in its wake an even deeper alienation of the major White denominations from Negro Protestantism.

The double tip-point in White Protestant withdrawal further accentuated the problem of desegregating local congregations. The initial retreat of high-status congregations left lower middle-class churches at the points of racial intersection. It is generally acknowledged that lower middle-class Whites have shown excessive prejudice against Negroes.[29] This is usually interpreted in terms of their marginal position; actually lower middle-class Whites pay disproportionately high rents in order to live in white-collar areas,[30] are extremely vulnerable to inflation, and fear anything which jeopardizes property values.[31] This vulnerable flank of Protestantism has repeatedly faced the Negro question. Higher-status congregations have shown no better acceptance of Negroes than lower middle-class Whites, and all hope for reconciliation dissolved with the retreat of stronger congregations from the central city. Lower middle-class Whites, left with dwindling congregations and shrinking church finances, formed the rearguard of the Protestant retreat from the central city; in fact, many middle-class Whites have kept a sense of social class identification with their more mobile compeers by resisting any attempts to desegregate the churches. Since many former residents continued for a time as members of the old church after moving away from the neighborhood, their less mobile associates maintained the life of the congregation unchanged out of loyalty to the church's former splendor.

The Protestant exodus can now be summarized: (1) *Roman Catholic immigrations* pushed Protestant congregations out of many areas of the central cities; to some extent, this was also true of Jewish immigrations at the turn of the century; these Protestant movements can be attributed to changes in the religious complexion of inner city areas, although the evidence suggests that many moves were premature and based on social class differences. These were almost inevitable movements for religious institutions whose principle of organization is the voluntary congregation; such churches move when the important members leave the area. (2) *Foreign-born Protestants* presented a different problem, since retreat in this instance caused a further fragmenting of Protestantism. (3) *The in-migration of White and Negro newcomers* also had a special effect; the Protestant retreat from these newcomers has created a schism in metropolitan religious life; the major White denominations are retreating to the suburban and satellite areas, while Negro and sectarian Protestantism are beginning to dominate central city areas. The major White denominations have moved toward exclusive identification with the White middle classes; in fact, they are insulating themselves geographically from the working-class people of the metropolitan areas. The net effect of population change has been an upgrading of the major denominations through social and physical insulation from the working classes.

Certain effects of the exodus on central city areas have been noted; the most important effect is an impoverishment of the Protestant ministry to the central city, which the growth of sectarian and Negro churches has not been able to offset. Thus, the areas of greatest social and physical need have enjoyed the least adequate ministries. Except for the large, high-status churches, ministerial tenure has been shortest in the central city churches; buildings have been poorest; programs, the least adequate. In general, the major denominations of White Protestantism have demonstrated a lack of relationship to the human struggle in the metropolis, except for occasional instances of institutional ministries.[32]

The story of metropolitan churches from 1870 to 1950 is the record of a desperate struggle for survival in the midst of rapid change. The average tenure of Protestant churches during this period was slightly over a score of years. It will probably be the same for the new and often elaborate buildings in suburbia unless the total organization of Protestantism changes. The metropolitan struggle for homogeneous neighborhoods infected the churches so that the intrusion of outsiders usually meant the collapse of both the neighborhood and the local religious groups. The pressures of rapid change turned congregations in upon themselves, so that they became more and more preoccupied with survival, less concerned with ministry to their communities. Neighborhoods became pools for recruiting members suitable to the social class level of the congregation; the metropolitan area became a field in which to choose prosperous sites for new church buildings.[33] Ministry assumed secondary importance, because population change made sheer survival as a parish or congregation highly problematic. Like men in a concentration camp who think only of food, these antique institutions lost touch with neighborhood and metropolis in their desperate struggle to survive. The parish and congregation were never designed for ministry in a rapidly changing metropolis; the attempt to maintain such institutions from 1870 to 1950 simply led to an exodus from the central city, and will lead in the next few decades to the collapse of the congregations which are being started each week.

We shall return to the problem of the congregation in the metropolis; it is essential in the present context, however, to recognize that the exodus was not a matter of bad faith or irresponsible leadership. It is naïve to think that men with better intentions can change the trend of events, when the best will in the world cannot make a congregation an instrument of ministry in a metropolis. What happened at the turn of the century is being repeated now in every major denomination. The attempt to perpetuate the local parish or congregation as a basic unit of the Christian Church is doomed to failure, although such local units will have to be the building blocks of a new and more adequate form of the Church in the metropolis. Before considering these aspects of the mission to the metropolis, however, the transformation in Protestantism which came with the exodus will have to be considered.

IDENTIFICATION WITH THE NEW MIDDLE CLASS

The disengagement of Christianity from the working classes has occurred several times before in the history of the churches, although the North African case is probably the most striking example. Christianity reached one of the peaks of its development in North Africa during the third and fourth centuries. St. Augustine, Bishop of Hippo, is undoubtedly the outstanding leader who emerged from North African Christianity; his thought set the course for the development of medieval Christianity, and he continues to be a rich source of philosophical and theological inspiration; nevertheless, within a few centuries North African Christianity disappeared without a trace. This collapse can certainly be attributed in part to the expansion of Islam; however, the core of the problem was the identification of North African Christianity with the upper social classes. The churches became centers of upper-class culture; consequently they lacked widespread support among the people. When Islam swept across North Africa, it erased Christianity.[34] Where Christianity has become identified with upper-class élites, it has lacked a substantial base in the working population and has been unable to weather social change.

The Chinese case is somewhat similar. Christianity never became rooted among the agrarian population of China. Every development of Nestorian Christianity in China disappeared within a century. The attempt to re-establish Christianity in the nineteenth century now seems doomed to collapse under the pressures of agrarian communism. The cases of North Africa and China involved complex cultural changes and many special factors; nevertheless, the identification of Christianity with upper-class élites or special subcultures has occurred in history and has eventuated in the disappearance of Christianity within a matter of centuries.

The identification of Christianity with the middle and upper classes occurred in recent centuries in Western Europe. This seems to be the primary factor in the decline of Christian churches in Sweden, England, and France. Christianity has deep roots in these countries, but urbanization has undermined it for centuries.[35] Urban Christianity in Western Europe has been concentrated among the bourgeoisie and has been alienated from the working classes; it is not uncommon in these countries for participation in worship to include only 10 to 15 per cent of the total population.[36] The European situation is complicated by the existence of established churches, for nominal memberships conceal the paucity of participation; moreover, the situation has caused deep concern to Christian leadership in Europe. The disappearance of Christianity from these countries, as from North Africa, could easily occur under the impact of a radical social revolution; for the moment, Christianity is resting its case with the bourgeoisie.

American Christianity does not seem to be following the European pattern. The major denominations in America give evidence of a growth which would seem to belie the foregoing analysis of the identification of Protestantism with the middle and upper social classes. One would expect an attenuation of membership in the major denominations, if the sloughing off of lower-class membership actually occurred between 1870 and 1950.[37] The seemingly contradictory picture—identification of the churches with middle and upper classes and increasing numerical strength—deserves special consideration, since it sets a pattern for the future of major denominations in their ministry to the metropolis. The American situation, in other words, presents certain unique characteristics which distinguish it from the North African and Western European developments.

The growth of the major denominations, despite losses in the central city areas, can be accounted for largely by the expansion of the middle classes since 1870. The mobility of Protestant churches made it possible for them to capitalize on this increase in the size of the middle class. For example, in St. Louis in 1923 four fifths of the population of the growing suburb of Webster Groves were members of Protestant churches as compared to the one-third Protestant membership in the city.[38] The losses incurred by major denominations in their movement away from the central city areas were more than offset by gains in the middle-class areas.

Central city losses and suburban gains of the major denominations conceal a fundamental change in the character of the Protestant constituency. A new middle class was emerging between 1870 and 1950, and it was this new middle-class population that was recruited during the Protestant exodus; consequently, the growth of the major denominations was a new phenomenon in Christianity. The character of this growth can be best understood in terms of concurrent changes in American industry.

Toward the end of the nineteenth century, industrial enterprises underwent a radical change; small businesses gave way to large, complicated industrial organizations, an expansion made possible by improved techniques of communication and engineering, which led in turn to more efficient organization of the labor force. The industrial revolution had originally applied power and organization to the fabrication of materials; specialization of work made it possible to distribute tasks within a manufacturing plant and improve the efficiency of production; nevertheless, labor was not organized according to highly standardized procedures and considerable scope remained for individual responsibility in operation. A workman had to use his own discretion in many phases of his work. Large-scale organization, on the other hand, requires more and more minute specification of operations and extremely careful organization of the various activities of men and women within an enterprise. This technological revolution in the organization of work occurred at the turn of the century and made possible the growth of gigantic industries.[39]

Many other factors such as incorporation, availability of capital, inventions of new processes, and improvement in transportation contributed to the growth of large industry. The important aspect of this development for the churches was the expansion of nonmanual occupations made possible by the development of large enterprise; a new middle class of propertyless managers, salesmen, office workers, engineers, technical specialists, and merchandisers came into existence. In more recent years, the growth of large organizations has become common in many fields of endeavor; medical, educational, and charitable institutions are now colossal enterprises with enormous staffs of nonmanual operatives; in fact, many lawyers and doctors now work in such organizations. Special fields of public relations, advertising, mass media communications, and governmental administration have followed the same path. The growth of population, the size and complexity of industrial establishments, and the growing bureaucratic structure of government have enormously increased the numbers who are employed in nonmanual occupations.[40]

This "white-collar pyramid," as C. Wright Mills so aptly called it, reaches from the lowest ranks of clerical help to high professional and governmental posts. The labor movement alone has created a huge force of nonmanual specialists who handle administrative, fiscal, and clerical problems. Every advance in technological control eliminates manual labor and increases the demand for technically skilled operatives; consequently, the work of foremen and skilled workers in modern industry is quite different from the traditional labor of the factory; in terms of income and type of work, skilled workers and foremen can often be ranked more accurately with the middle classes. The distinction between white and blue collar fails to deal adequately with the significance of this technological revolution in occupations, since education and skill are the principal marks of the new middle class, and skilled workers tend to be middle class in orientation.[41]

The pyramid of white-collar and technically skilled occupations expanded steadily after 1870; the new middle class alone grew from less than 1 per cent of the nonfarm work force in 1870 to 25 per cent of the labor force by 1940.[42] If one uses income figures to estimate this growing band of the middle classes, the figures are roughly comparable, although they reflect larger membership in the skilled labor force. Between 1929 and 1953 the middle-income group moved from 12 per cent of American families who shared 25 per cent of the total cash income to 35 per cent who shared 42 per cent of the total cash income of the nation.[43] Middle-class occupational groups and middle-income groups are not identical, but they provide estimates of the size of the prosperous middle which has emerged in the last eighty years. *Table 1* gives an estimate of the growth of the middle class since 1870; expectations are for a rapid increase in this group.

TABLE 1.   Percentage of Nonfarm Work Force in
Middle-Class Occupations, 1870–1950.[44]

Date	Estimated Percentage
1870	10%
1910	25%
1920	28.6%
1930	31%
1940	32%
1950	35% +

The expanding middle class swelled the movement of population to the suburban and satellite areas of the metropolitan communities from 1870 to 1950. The influx of unskilled labor from foreign lands and rural areas replenished the lower ranks in the labor force and crowded the central areas of the cities; those who could move up a few rungs on the economic ladder moved to better residential areas and adopted a middle-class style of life.[45] The congregations of the major denominations followed a similar path and concentrated their recruitment among the families of this emerging middle class. *Table* 2 gives some indication of the character of the growth of Protestantism from 1870 to 1950.

TABLE 2. Percentage of Protestants to Total
Population by Decades, 1870–1950.[46]

Year	Estimated Percentage
1870	12%
1880	13%
1890	14%
1900	24%
1910	28%
1930	28%
1940	28.7%
1950	33.8%

A few remarks about *Table* 2 may help to interpret the actual state of recruitment in the major denominations. There are two periods of marked growth in Protestant membership—1870–1900 and 1940–1950. The period 1870–1900 can be explained by the development of more accurate estimates of membership through the work of the Bureau of the Census and also by the expansion of nominal memberships in the urban areas; moreover, these figures were expanded through immigration. The major denominations have not gained members in excess of basic population growth since 1940, so they have merely held their own during this period. The major denominations have enjoyed an expansion of membership roughly proportional to the expansion of population. Moreover, the increases in membership from 1940 to 1950, and even later, are concentrated largely in the sectarian and fundamentalist churches.

The major denominations have been losing membership in rural areas during much of this period. These losses were largely a consequence of the drop in middle-class farmers as a proportion of the middle-class labor force from 62 per cent to 23 per cent between 1870 and 1940.[47] The major denominations were recruiting largely in the metropolitan areas to compensate for their losses in the rural areas, although, as has been noted, their metropolitan strength was only 46 per cent of their constituency by 1953.[48] Even notable gains of the major denominations in suburban areas barely offset losses in rural and central city areas. The picture of a religious revival, however real it may be, should not obscure this factual picture of the development of the major denominations: they have been running full speed in order to stay in the same place; they have built and planned and schemed in order to remain at dead center. The appearance of growth turns out to be a stable percentage of total population. The stable percentage conceals a total turnover in the type of constituency of the major denominations: from memberships drawn largely from rural and urban working and entrepreneurial middle classes the churches are rapidly becoming dominated by the bureaucratic middle class.

Table 1 makes clear why it was possible for the major denominations to go through the exodus and identify so completely with the middle classes without suffering obvious losses in membership; in fact, with the middle classes still growing in proportion to the total labor force, middle-class Protestantism can continue to conceal rural and central city losses. The major denominations only attracted a segment of the metropolitan middle classes, but what strength they gained came from these ranks, and the middle classes were expanding rapidly enough to sustain the membership figures. The religious revival has been principally a middle-class affair for the major denominations; so much so, in fact, that actual increases in membership over population growth have been confined to the left-wing churches of Protestantism. In general, it would be fair to say that the major denominations have cut themselves away from a membership twice their present strength by identifying with their middle-class members rather than ministering to the entire metropolitan area. The disastrous consequences of their exodus were temporarily offset by the expansion of the middle classes.

The full import of the exodus becomes evident when one considers the internal transformation which was occurring simultaneously in Protestant ranks: the working-class constituency of the major denominations was being sloughed off during the outward movement of Protestant congregations; Protestant growth barely exceeded population growth from 1910 to 1930, although the lower birth rates among families of the major denominations indicate accessions over and above normal gains; meanwhile, the ranks of the middle class were expanding. The major denominations did not really grow during this period: *they changed the character of their constituency*; in fact, they compensated for losses in the central city areas by recruitment among the new middle classes of the suburbs.[49] This internal transformation could come about without evident losses in Protestant membership, although the actual losses were considerable. If the major denominations had held or increased their memberships in central city areas while recruiting and expanding on the fringes of the cities, one can assume that their actual memberships would now be considerably above the present figures. This is not a matter of wishful thinking. The major denominations abandoned the residents of the central city areas in the course of the exodus, and furthermore, they failed to recruit the rural constituency who were migrating to central city areas. What they were losing by emigration from rural areas, they were abandoning in the central city areas.

A significant fact about the transformation in Protestant membership between 1870 and 1950 is the character of the new middle class, for this group makes up a substantial part of the metropolitan constituency of Protestantism. The new middle class is distinguished by its means of livelihood. The middle class of the nineteenth century was comprised largely of those whose livelihoods were gained on farms or in enterprises which they owned in whole or part. It was a property-holding group. The farmer, small entre-

preneur, and small merchandiser filled the ranks of the middle class
and made up a major element in Protestantism; for example, in the
1820s, 80 per cent of the people earned their living by working on
property which they owned, as against 20 per cent today.[50] The
middle classes are now as much expropriated as the proletariat.
Most of them are job-holders, dependent upon someone else's enterprise for a livelihood. The new white-collar group is comprised
increasingly of the bureaucratic middle class, whose lives are shaped
by adjustments to the demands of big organization; whether they
are clerks, stenographers, or managers they are dependent almost
entirely upon their skill and capacity to hold a job. Manipulators of
people and paper, marketers of personality and mental skills, merchants of words and artists in interpersonal skill, they are better
educated, better fed, and better paid than any occupational group
of comparable size in history. The new middle class is the organization class *par excellence*. It is also the constituency of the new
metropolitan Protestantism.

EMERGENCE OF THE NEW PROTESTANTISM

From 1870 to 1950 the major denominations of Protestantism
underwent a twofold transformation: (1) they decentralized their
strong congregations to the suburban and satellite areas—an outward movement traced in the Protestant exodus; (2) they changed
the character of their constituency, since losses among the rural
middle class and urban working classes were offset by gains among
the new suburban middle class.[51] We can assume that they maintained contact with the remnants of the old middle class, although
this *lumpen* bourgeoisie suffered financial losses in this period.

Why these new middle-class groups have gravitated to the
churches in the United States more than in the industrialized nations of Western Europe is difficult to explain. It could be argued
that metropolitan expansion in the United States has been much
more rapid and disrupting for middle-class people. This argument
would lend credence to the notion that the middle classes have
been seeking deeper roots and a firmer base in continuing values
through relationships with the churches. It would also account for

the increasing religious interest in the more Americanized and middle-class ranks of Roman Catholicism. Western Europe is also enjoying industrial expansion and increase in the bureaucratic middle classes, but these new elements find more stable patterns of life there. This interpretation of the American situation would also confirm our previous emphasis on the *rapidity* of change rather than the *fact* of social change in the metropolitan area. The annihilation of all roots for middle-class people in less than a generation can have disturbing effects unless there are some stabilizing points of reference. The attachment of these groups to congregational and parochial life can be understood in terms of the peculiar interests and needs of the emerging middle class. An appraisal of this bond between the new middle class and the Protestant congregation provides a fundamental clue to the potential of the major denominations for a ministry to the metropolis.

THREE

The Churches as Fellowships and Missions

The mark of the primitive church was social inclusiveness—rich and poor, Jew and gentile, slave and free. The characteristic of the church of the metropolis is exclusiveness. The exclusive congregations of the major denominations advertise themselves as "friendly churches" and put a premium on the friendly handclasp, warm cup of coffee, and something for everyone to do. Despite this warmth of sentiment, the typical congregation is a very homogeneous social and economic grouping.

Much of this exclusiveness comes about "naturally." The style of life, manner of dress, form of worship, appointments, windows, clerical garb, and even the coffee hour serve to include some and exclude others.[1] There is nothing conscious or intentional about such exclusion, although we have already seen in the exodus that strong, unconscious forces have been driving a wedge between the major denominations and the blue-collar ranks. The net effect of the denominational style is a congregation in which conformity and even uniformity become the marks of membership.

Another feature of the denominational church is active affability. The new middle classes who have been consistently recruited by the major denominations place a premium on affability. It is an occupational characteristic of white-collar people, whose lives are spent in situations where promotions and even holding a job depend upon "getting along" with others. The sanctification of "getting along" is generalized in American culture, but particularly pronounced in the white-collar world.[2] Contrast to the blue-collar world is nowhere more pronounced than in the difference between a white-collar association and a blue-collar union—the former ostracizing those who engender conflict, the latter thriving on it. The active affability of the typical denominational church contrasts notably with the mentality and environment of blue-collar life.[3] This stress on affability shows up repeatedly in appraisals of the minister's role by laymen; when asked what is the most important asset of a good minister, the majority of laymen will score personality. Healthy glands and an attractive smile have come to be the necessary, if not the sufficient, conditions of a "successful" ministry. This is true largely because of the peculiar role played by congregational life in the whole economy of middle-class life.

The conformity of congregation and minister to the middle-class style of life reflects a deep current of conformism in American culture. The churches are bound to this conformist trend so long as they confine their religious units—whether parishes or congregations —to local residential areas, since the neighborhood is now the center of conformity in American culture. The local neighborhood could not exert this conformist pressure until it was possible to separate place of work and place of residence. Once this segregation came about through rapid transportation and construction of large, centralized plants, the local neighborhood could become a center for the cultivation of a social style. The sundering of communities of production and consumption may well prove to be the most important single change produced by the industrial revolution. A religious association is quickly assimilated to this new role of the residential community as long as its center of gravity is residential. Only a century ago, a residential community intersected with many other kinds of exchanges and productive activities. Today, city planners consider the existence of nonresidential uses in a residential area to be slum-producing features of the district. A new kind of fellowship emerges in a neighborhood when it ceases to reflect the inequalities and interdependencies of human life and becomes an image of the homogeneity of a particular group.

The congregation seems to be free of such local bonds in the metropolis, for it builds around the commitment of a fellowship rather than the social identity of a neighborhood group. The congregation is quite distinct from the local parish, which is grounded in locale. This is true as a broad distinction, but the net effect has made little difference to the conformism of congregations. Even though the congregation is free of its locale, it is built even more exclusively around the identity of a specific social class than the local parish.

The congregation has only its own fellowship as a point of inter-section for its life of faith and obedience. In a stable community such a fellowship can represent a confessing, believing, and obedi-ent sector of the total community. In a shifting metropolis this fel-lowship is prey to the panicky search for stability, detaching itself from the sense of ministry or mission. It would be difficult to choose between parish or congregation as religious forms in a metropolis, for both types are extremely vulnerable to the trends to residential exclusiveness. Furthermore, freedom from locale in the congrega-tional form is largely a myth, as can be seen by the failure of all congregations in central cities except a few with high prestige and a few that specialize in preaching or bizarre theologies. The new role of residential communities in American life has created a new kind of conformist religious life, a conformity that shapes the fel-lowship and mission of the churches. The new meaning of residence and the new pattern of Christian fellowship are inextricably inter-woven. The break in this iron law of conformity will only occur when the residential anchorage is shifted. Before considering such new directions, however, it is essential to grasp the significance of residential association in the economy of middle-class culture.

ECONOMIC INTEGRATION OF CONGREGATIONS

Various images of religious organization have shaped the Chris-tian imagination through the centuries. The New Testament is re-plete with such images: St. Paul speaks of the Church as the Body of Christ and the Household of Faith; St. Peter speaks of the Church as People of God, Royal Priesthood, and Temple. The idea of the Church as the Body of Christ in medieval times connoted a family, a brotherhood, or a household. The Reformation overturned several features of medieval Christianity; consequently, traditional images of the Church underwent transformation. The Reformed image of the Church was that of a gathered congregation—a com-munity of believers. American Puritanism altered the image of the gathered congregation to a classroom; American Protestantism re-flected this classroom mentality in its church architecture and liturgical practice. Preaching, instruction, and the open Book were the marks of this tradition. The idolatries, indulgences, and corruptions of Rome had been swept from the temple. New England Protestantism produced an austere image of teacher and taught, truth and obedience, faith and hard work. The congregation of believers was a core of disciplined, committed, and hardy saints.

A new image of the Church has begun to emerge with the appearance of the new middle class. It is this new image which concerns us here, for it shapes the possibilities for a ministry to the metropolis. The new image of the Church is a reflection of the dominant principle of association in American life, *economic integration:* people in a metropolitan area associate with one another on the basis of similar occupations, prestige, income, residence, and style of life.

Most personal associations today occur in relation to family life and residential neighborhood; families seldom associate with occupational friends of the head of the household, unless they are also neighbors; in fact, father's associates on the job may have little or no contacts with him in his private life. Economic integration means that families associate with other families whose residence, income, and style of life reflect a comparable position on the economic ladder. The rungs of the economic ladder dictate the eligible candidates for human association in metropolitan areas.

The nature of economic integration is illustrated by the features of the "American Dilemma" in racial relations. The dilemma arises because the American ideology affirms that free and open competition in the market decides man's fate; every man should have an equal opportunity to win his place in the sun.[4] In principle, happiness is open to anyone with the ability to perform adequately. In the American creed, land, labor, commodities, and capital are subject to the competitive market.[5] The important inequalities, according to the creed, are those of ability. If a man has the capacity, he can achieve any rank, including the presidency; the legend of Abraham Lincoln appeals profoundly to Americans because it portrays this principle of performance and reward in its most dramatic form. Despite the American creed, however, Negroes, Jews, and other minority groups experience varying degrees of exclusion from the market place; handicapped in business competition, they often succeed financially only to find themselves excluded from residential areas, clubs, etc. Gunnar Myrdal referred to the Negro problem as the American Dilemma because the Negro was almost totally excluded from opportunities, jobs, adequate schooling, and decent living conditions; consequently, the principle of open competition proved inapplicable to the Negro. The American community accepts the principle of open competition and economic integration as sacred.[6]

This sanctification of competition stresses individual achievements in the struggle for rewards. Inherited privileges still make a big difference in this competitive system, but they do not create walls of exclusion except for certain groups who become objects of discrimination. Economic integration of neighborhoods is the residential reward for achievement in the open market; those who succeed are privileged to live in better homes and among others of similar color who have done equally well. Communities are integrated by strata in the occupational world, with finer adjustments of inclusion or exclusion according to special criteria such as ethnic background, religion, and race. The right to "belong" in human communities is, thus, dependent upon performances in the economic world.[7] Moreover, the rule of the market is universal.[8]

The separation of residence and place of work—generally speaking, an entirely new phenomenon of the industrial world—has given a peculiar twist to association by likeness. When transportation was slow and difficult, people lived near one another on the basis of family relationships and mutual need. For example, antebellum areas of Southern cities still have mixed residence of Negroes and Whites. The Negroes live near to the Whites because they were the slave and serving group. By contrast, Negro residence in Montgomery, Alabama, was sufficiently separated from the White residential areas to make access on foot extremely difficult. During the bus strike in Montgomery, many White families found themselves in difficult straits without help from the laundress, maid, nurse, or general helper. Bus, car, trolley, and subway have transformed the role of residential association. Economic dependence seldom serves any longer to maintain the relationships between rich and poor, strong and weak, leader and led. The more successful can build a suburban curtain around themselves and still be served by the poor on an hourly basis; that is, they can manage such insulation if there are no bus strikes.

The desire to insulate a residential area against poorer people or even against those who are more successful is partly a consequence of the unfreezing of positions in the competitive way of life. Again, the ante-bellum South illustrates a pattern which has prevailed in greater or lesser degree in many parts of the world during most of recorded history. Landowners or small entrepreneurs in the slave economy of the South had a clear position of superiority over the slaves. Even the pressed Whites without land were socially above the enslaved Negroes, although their economic position was seriously jeopardized by the slave economy. Mixed residence offers no serious threat to the prestige of those in superior positions when superordination and subordination are well established and every gesture, mode of personal address, and charitable act discloses the superiority of the owner and the dependence of his inferiors. Once these stable ranks are shaken by shifting gains in an open market, who is up and who is down cannot be simply settled by the hat-in-hand gesture or the trip to the kitchen door to make a request. Post-bellum sections of Southern cities are more or less segregated and serve as an interesting index of the new status of the Negro after Emancipation; not yet treated as an equal, he was no longer owned. The inferiority of the Negro no longer had the support of unquestioned legal-economic sanctions; one could no longer afford residential proximity to one whose inferiority was uncertain. The shift in residential patterns came slowly in the South after the Emancipation, but the new patterns of segregated residence were built from the emerging equality of Negro and White. That equality is yet to be realized in many areas of Southern culture, but the very possibility shifted the pattern of residential association.

Association by likeness is a familiar phenomenon in human society; hence, residential association by likeness of social and economic position is hardly a strange development in the metropolis.

It seems the most natural thing in the world, and it *is* natural in the usual sense of the word. The new feature of residential association in metropolitan areas is the sundering of economic interdependence from personal association. The most obvious illustration of this commonplace is the stripping of leadership from many areas of the central cities. The men and women who are practiced and skilled in the organization of affairs now live on the outer edges of the metropolis. There are, of course, many more leaders in lower social ranks than most people realize, but much of this leadership is unskilled and unorganized. The fact is, nonetheless, that those who assume leadership in most enterprises today have segregated themselves from any contact with those who execute their orders in the occupational world. These so-called leaders have little idea of how their employees live. The mutual dependence of economic life which has traditionally bound families together no longer serves to integrate the lives and residences of rich and poor, leader and led, strong and weak. Residential association is now built almost exclusively around similarity in economic rank. Once interdependence of human life is denied in the residential sphere, men and women seek the safety of associating with those on a similar rung of the economic ladder.

The sundering of residential association from the interdependence of human life can be explained by the ease with which residence can be segregated from place of work. The widespread use of the automobile and the construction of the freeway are making this separation of bed and job almost universal in the American metropolis. If present trends in residential association continue, it should be possible to locate families in social rank very precisely simply by residential area. At present, differences in education, ethnic origin, and even occupational position make simple predictions from residential areas rather inaccurate, but the trend is toward increasing homogeneity of families in residential areas despite talk about "mixed" redevelopment areas and the return to the central city. Only the widespread building of smaller units of public housing in various parts of the metropolis and the distribution of lower middle-income housing on similar lines could offset this trend to homogeneity of residential areas. There are very few indications that these counteractive trends toward metropolitan interdependence in residential association are gaining much support. Association by likeness and economic integration of residential areas is the dominant motif. Consumer communities are conformist and exclusive. Residential association becomes, thus, a counteractive force to the heterogeneity of metropolitan peoples.

Since churches organize their congregations or parishes primarily around residential neighborhoods and secondarily around family ties, congregations can be expected to mirror the economic ladder which determines place of residence. Each congregation will tend to become a cluster of people of like social and economic position. Ethnic and racial characteristics will identify particular congregations. Long-standing ties of old-country denominations such as Swedish, Danish, or Norwegian Lutheranism become marks of social and economic exclusiveness in ethnic guise. Swedish Lutheranism becomes another name for homogeneity by remote ethnic origin and present similarity of economic rank. In a society that sunders residential association from economic interdependence, creating a new social pattern of insulated enclaves, the churches will tend to be expressions of these insulated enclaves so long as their principle of organization is the congregation or parish in the residential area. This is, in fact, the case. Metropolitan parishes and congregations are organized by similarity of social and economic rank; they are prime examples of economic integration under religious auspices.[9] In fact, churches are more homogeneous than their locale. The interdependence of the human community is less apparent in the gathering of worshipers than in the neighborhood itself. The service of worship proclaims the sacredness of association by similarity in economic performance, symbolizing the insulation of one social rank against another rather than mutual dependence of rich and poor, insider and outsider, strong and weak, leader and led.

A new image of the Church is emerging in the contemporary world, an image created by the domination of contemporary life by economic activities. The Church is now a reflection of the economic ladder. Ascent on this ladder is validated by escalation to congregations of higher social and economic rank. For every rung on the ladder there is an appropriate congregation, with ushers of slightly more refined dress and somewhat more cultivated ladies' affairs. Such small stylistic differences are the bread of life in a society dedicated to the service of productivity. The rising standard of living is imaged in the stratification of churches and neighborhoods. As long as the basic unit of Christianity is a residentially organized congregation or parish, the average church will be a reflection of one or another of the rungs on the economic ladder.

The most obvious example of conformity in the denominational churches is recruitment from the white-collar groups. The difference between blue collar and white collar is partly one of point of view, as we have seen in the discussion of the exodus. Foremen and skilled workers may be middle class in orientation even though their work is manual. If these workers are in the middle-income brackets, as most of them are, and if they are antiunion and opposed to government interference in such matters as public health or housing, one can be reasonably confident that they will be affiliated with congregations of the major denominations. Being middle class is more than simply a matter of keeping away from grease and dirt. One can be *in* grease and not *of* it, and this is characteristically true of church members in the major denominations who are recruited from the blue-collar ranks. One way in which the major denominations have mirrored the economic ladder is by recruiting almost exclusively from the middle classes and welcoming those from the blue-collar ranks whose hearts were set on things above.[10]

Thus far, we have considered economic integration as a consequence of the separation of bed from job. The practice of organizing congregations around residential groupings, on this basis, would be an inevitable result of social change. The case for economic integration of congregations is much stronger than historical accident, although these accidental elements were undoubtedly present. Congregations are explicitly organized around similarity in social and economic rank; in fact, their survival generally depends upon the degree to which they can maintain likeness in their memberships. A few highbrows and a few lowbrows can be thrown into the congregational mix, but the core group has to be drawn from similar occupation, income group, educational level, ethnic background, and residential level if the congregation is to survive. As we shall observe subsequently in this analysis, the emergence of the organization church represents the development of a flexible means to create a congregation of "like people" from the flotsam of the metropolis. The development of innumerable subsidiary organizations in the churches has also provided a mechanism for distributing people into groupings which are somewhat more homogeneous than the total congregation; thus, the lower middle-class women can spend their time baking and sewing, while the middle-middle women with their up-and-coming ways can attend to dessert bridges and flower arangements, foregoing brownies and fruitcake for tinseled decorations and elaborate table arrangements. There can be peace in the house when such differences of style in the middle-class ranks complement one another by finding outlets in different organizational activities.

The chaotic crisscrossing of worshipers on Sunday morning as they seek out the churches of their choice is an expression of the principle of economic integration. Protestants pass by churches of their own denomination which are higher or lower in social status than their own in order to worship with their economic peers.[11] Downtown churches of high prestige draw members from the whole metropolis and distribute the members in homogeneous groupings, while Protestants of the lower middle class who live nearby attend elsewhere.[12] Churchgoing in a metropolis is determined by personal preference, denominational affiliation, and similarity in social and economic status. In case of doubt, similarity of social and economic status wins hands down for most members. Studies of Protestant attendance disclose a maze of churchgoing patterns in the city, but the key to this maze is the search by middle-class people for socially homogeneous groupings, and the key to homogeneity is economic level. A Protestant church of a major denomination can prosper in a deteriorated neighborhood provided it can locate a cluster of socially homogeneous white-collar people within a mile of the church building. Many of the churches of the major denominations which have survived in central city areas have done so on this basis; in one way and another they have been able to attract a socially homogeneous group.[13]

The key to life in any group is the factor that determines its survival and continuity in a changing world. A family collapses when the love and fidelity between husband and wife dissolve. A state collapses when the government cannot protect its territory and/or maintain order. A Protestant congregation collapses when it cannot recruit a socially homogeneous membership. Every social group depends on numerous factors to sustain its life; each group, however, has its key to life, without which it ceases to be; this is its principle of life. One would expect the principle of life in a congregation to be faith, but in the major denominations it is social homogeneity or economic integration.

Let us consider a lower-class area of the metropolis: a congregation of one of the major denominations meets in this area; less than one half of the members still live in the neighborhood of the church building;[14] few of the local residents attend, although their children pass it every day on their way to school and see other Protestants attending the church on Sundays; very few of the Protestant residents of the area go to any church; those who do attend churches scatter among lower-class congregations in other areas and in neighborhood sect groups. In general, churchgoing is disproportionately low in such an area; in fact, two or more times as many residents of middle-class areas attend churches.[15]

Why do Protestants in this lower-class area not attend local churches of the major denominations? Are they less religious than people in the suburbs? Has God hardened their hearts so that they do not respond? Studies of religious activity indicate that people who are lonely and under stress turn to religion.[16] These people are isolated and under stress, and yet they do not attend this church. It seems reasonable to assume that they are disposed to be religious; in fact, proliferation of sects in central city areas would bear out this assumption. Therefore, we can assume that the lower-class residents avoid this church because it is socially a middle-class congregation. We can also assume that those who do attend this church are neither more nor less religious by nature; they attend the church because it is on their social class level. In general, religious interest seems to exist in all parts of the metropolis; congregational membership, however, is another thing. A congregation survives only if it can sustain a socially homogeneous membership; that is, when it can preserve economic integration. Religious faith can be considered a *necessary* condition of membership in a congregation, since the decision to join a worshiping group requires some motive force, but faith is not a *sufficient* condition for joining; the presence of other members of similar social and economic level is the *sufficient* condition.

The breakdown of social homogeneity in inner city areas and the spread of inner city blight account for the decline of central city churches. Central cities reveal two adverse features for the major denominations: (1) central cities tend to be areas of residence for lower social classes; (2) central cities tend to be more heterogeneous in social composition. The central city areas, in other words, exhibit the two characteristics which violate the life principle of congregations of the major denominations: they have too few middle-class people; they mix middle-class people with lower-class residents. Central city areas have become progressively poorer locales for the major denominations since the exodus of middle-class people from most central cities. With few exceptions, the major denominations are rapidly losing their hold on the central city.[17]

The key to Protestant development, therefore, is economic integration of the nucleus of the congregation. Members of higher and lower social status often cluster around this nucleus, so that Protestant figures on social class give the impression of spread over all social classes; but this is deceptive, for the core of membership is concentrated in a single social and economic stratum. The congregation perishes when it is no longer possible to replenish that core from the neighborhood; moreover, residential mobility is so high in metropolitan areas that churches have to recruit constantly in their core stratum in order to survive; they can lose higher- and lower-status members from the church without collapsing, but they need adequate recruits for the core stratum in order to preserve economic integration. The congregation is first and foremost an economic peer group; it is secondarily a believing and worshiping fellowship. If it were primarily a believing fellowship, it would recruit believers from all social and economic ranks, something which most congregations of the New Protestantism (with a few notable exceptions) have not been able to do. They survive only when they can recruit social and economic peers.[18]

The vulnerability of Protestant congregations to social differences has often been attributed to the "folksy spirit" of Protestant religious life; in fact, a contrast is often drawn in this regard with the "impersonal" Roman Catholic parish.[19] We have seen that the folksy spirit is confined to economic peers; consequently, the vulnerability to social difference should not be attributed to the stress on personal community in Protestant congregations; actually, there is little evidence of such personal community in Protestant congregations, as we shall see in another connection. The vulnerability of Protestantism to social differences stems from the peculiar role of the new religious style in middle-class life, where the congregation is a vehicle of social and economic group identity and must conform, therefore, to the principle of economic integration. This fact is evident in the recruitment of new members.

MISSION AS CO-OPTATION

The rule of economic integration in congregational life can be seen in the missionary outreach of the major denominations. There is much talk in theological circles about the "Church as Mission" and the "Church's Mission"; theologians have been stressing the fact that the Church does not exist for its own sake but as a testimony in the world for the healing of the world.[20] A crucial question, therefore, is what evangelism and mission actually mean in metropolitan Protestantism. If economic integration really shapes congregational life, then evangelism should be a process of extending economic integration. The task of a congregation would be defined, according to economic integration, as the work of co-opting individuals and families of similar social and economic position to replenish the nuclear core of the congregation. (Co-optation means to choose by joint action in order to fill a vacancy; it can also mean the assimilation of centers of power from an environment in order to strengthen an organization.)[21] In a mobile society, congregational health depends on a constant process of recruitment; this recruitment, however, must follow the pattern of economic integration or it will disrupt the congregation; therefore, the recruitment or missionary outreach of the congregation will be co-optation rather than proclamation—like elements will have to be assimilated.

Evangelism and congregational outreach have not been carefully studied in the churches; one study in Pittsburgh, however, has illuminated the situation. In a sample of new members of Pittsburgh churches, almost 60 per cent were recruited by initial "contacts with friendly members."[22] If we add to these contacts with friendly members the "contacts with an organization of the church" (11.2 per cent of the cases), then a substantial two thirds of all recruitment is through friendly contact. On the surface, this seems a sound approach to Christian mission: members of the congregation show by their friendly attitudes that they care for new people; the new people respond in kind by joining the church.

Missionary outreach by friendly contact looks somewhat different when one reflects on what is known about friendly contact in metropolitan neighborhoods; the majority of such contacts are with people of similar social and economic position; association by level of achievement is the dominant principle of informal relations.[23] This means that the antennae of the congregation are extended into the community, picking up the wave lengths of those who will fit into the social and economic level of the congregation; the mission of the church is actually a process of informal co-optation; the lay ministry is a means to recruit like-minded people who will strengthen the social class nucleus of the congregation. Churches can be strengthened through this process of co-optation so long as the environs of the church provide a sufficient pool of people who can fit the pattern of economic integration; once the pool of recruits diminishes, the congregation is helpless—friendly contacts no longer keep it going.

The transmutation of mission to co-optation is further indicated by the insignificance of educational activities, worship, preaching, and publicity in reaching new members. The proclamation of the churches is almost totally confined to pastoral contacts by the clergy (17.3 per cent of new members) and friendly contacts by members (over two thirds if organizational activities are included). Publicity accounted for 1.1 per cent of the initial contacts with new members. In general, friendly contact with a member followed by contact with a clergyman will account for a major share of recruitment by the churches, making it quite evident that the extension of economic integration through co-optation is the principal form of mission in the contemporary church; economic integration and co-optation are the two methods by which Protestants associate with and recruit from the neighborhood. The inner life of congregations will prosper so long as like-minded people of similar social and economic level can fraternize together; the outer life of congregations—the suitability of the environment to their survival —will be propitious so long as the people in the area are of the same social and economic level as the membership. Economic integration ceases when the social and economic statuses in an area become too mixed or conflict with the status of the congregation. In a rapidly changing society congregations will run into difficulties repeatedly, since such nice balances of economic integration are hard to sustain in the metropolis for more than a single generation. The fact that metropolitan churches of the major denominations have moved approximately every generation for the last hundred years becomes somewhat more intelligible in the light of this struggle to maintain economic balance. The expense of this type of organization in religious life, when one recalls the number of city churches which deteriorated beyond repair before being abandoned, raises fundamental questions about the principle of Protestant survival in a mobile society; nonetheless, the prevalence of economic integration in congregations illumines the nature of the Protestant development.

It was observed in the introductory chapter that metropolitan life had split into two trends—expanding interdependence on an impersonal basis and growing exclusiveness in local communal groupings. These trends seem to be working at cross-purposes in the metropolis. Residential associations struggle to insulate themselves against intrusions. The motifs of impersonal interdependence and insulation of residential communities have polarized; the schism between central city and suburb, Negro and White, blue collar and white collar can be viewed as symptomatic of this deeper polarization of trends in the metropolis. It now becomes evident that the denominational church is intimately involved with the economy of middle-class culture, for it serves to crystallize the social class identity of middle-class residential groupings. The accelerated pace of metropolitan changes has accentuated the drive to conformity in congregations of the major denominations. This conformity represents a desperate attempt to stabilize a hopelessly unstable environment. More than creatures of metropolitan forces, the churches have taken the lead in counteracting the interdependence of metropolitan life, crystallizing and perpetuating the stratification of peoples, giving form to the struggle for social homogeneity in a world of heterogeneous peoples.

Since American life is committed above all to productivity and a higher standard of economic life, the countervailing forces of residential and religious exclusiveness have fought a desperate, rearguard action against the expanding interdependence of the metropolis. Consumer communities have suffered at the hands of the productive interests. Negroes, Puerto Ricans, and rural newcomers are slowly making their way into the cities. Soon they will fight their way into the lower middle-class suburbs, and the churches will experience the same decay and rebuilding cycle which has characterized their history for a century. The identification of the basic unit of religious organization—the parish or congregation—with a residential area is self-defeating in a modern metropolis, for it simply means the closing of an iron trap on the outreach of the Christian fellowship and the transmutation of mission to co-optation. Mission to the metropolis contradicts survival of the congregation in the residential community, because the middle classes are fighting metropolitan interdependence with residential exclusion.

This interpretation of the role of residence in the economy of middle-class culture could lead to various projections for the churches. It could be argued that any fellowship which centers in residential neighborhoods is doomed to become an expression of the panic for stable identity among the middle classes. It could be argued that only such neighborhoods can sustain religious activity, since worship presupposes some local stabilities. Whatever projection one makes, the striking fact about congregational and parochial life is the extent to which it is a vehicle of the social identity of middle-class people.[24]

Attention will be given in the next chapter to the style of association in the denominational churches; this style is characteristically an expression of the communal style of the middle classes.[25] The keynotes of this style are activism and emphasis on achievements in gaining self-esteem.[26] These values give direction to the life of the middle-class man or woman, dictating the methods of child rearing, determining the pattern of community participation, setting the style for the psychiatric treatment of middle-class illness, and informing the congregational life of the major denominations.[27] "Fellowship by likeness" and "mission by friendly contact" form the iron cage of denominational religion. Its contents are another matter, for they reveal the kinds of interests pursued by the congregation. What goes on in the cage will occupy our attention under the rubric of the organization church. An understanding of the new role of residential association in an industrial society serves to illuminate the forces which have fashioned the iron cage of conformity which imprisons the churches in their suburban captivity.

The perplexing question still remains as to why the middle classes turn to the churches as a vehicle of social identity when their clubs and charities should fill the same need. The local Republican club should serve as well as the local church. The search for identity in the churches seems to be a grasp for traditional symbols of stability by an uprooted and alienated social class; the religious interests of this group are an expression of an authentic search for values and stability in the rapidly changing milieu of an industrial and metropolitan world.

The new middle class is a traditionless group. Its position in the world is very uncertain; in fact, its sense of corporate identity, as an awareness of a continuing place in the world, is relatively weak. This politically powerless and economically dependent group has found in denominational life a means of establishing a tradition, a sense of continuity, and a confidence in the future.[28] This fact, more than any other, accounts for the marked religious interests of the new middle classes; their position in the world is validated through participation in congregational life. The only condition on which the denominational churches could provide a vehicle of social identity for the new middle class was by preserving a socially homogeneous congregation. The intrusion of outsiders from other social and economic levels would threaten that social identity; the admission of Negroes to White churches would undermine the confidence of the White membership in their own social and economic position; thus, the churches have succeeded in recruiting the middle classes by maintaining exclusive enclaves on the principle of economic integration and following the middle classes in their exodus from the central cities.

The paradox of the continued resistance of White Protestantism to desegregation of the churches can only be understood through awareness that the Protestant congregation is at once the confirmation of the economic-social identity of the middle classes and the basic principle of their sense of continuity in a changing world.[29] The Protestant congregation is not a "chummy fellowship" which can afford intimacy with Negroes. It is a collectivity which serves as a symbol of membership in the White middle class and as a guarantee that one has a future in this middle-class world. In the midst of rapid social change, this island of safety would be jeopardized by racial inclusiveness; it is the religious expression of the metropolitan principle of communal exclusiveness.

THE TASK OF MINISTRY

Denominational Protestantism is handicapped in the task of ministry in the metropolis, a fact recognized by many clergymen and laymen. It is commonplace in meetings on urban strategy to acknowledge the difficulty of the churches before the spreading blight of the inner city. There are, to be sure, clergymen and laymen who deny that denominational Protestantism is inadequate to this task. There are certain problems in the metropolitan ministry, however, which they cannot solve; the major denominations are helpless before social differences; they cannot sustain a ministry in an area of social disorganization; yet, this is the type of area that desperately needs their ministry. Denominational Protestantism is confounded by the racial problem; racial integration may occur slowly in the suburbs as a kind of economic integration, but the major denominations already foresee their death in the central city with the emerging Negro monopoly in the central cities.[30] These facts alone raise radical questions about the adequacy of denominational Protestantism; as presently constituted, Protestantism is fighting a losing battle to minister to the metropolis.

The real difficulty with denominational Protestantism is its arrested development as a form of the Church; this, at least, is the approach that will be taken to the problem in the subsequent discussion. The social organization of the major denominations has been malleable to the particular interests of the new middle classes —their search for exclusive enclaves of social identity. This is pathology, because true identity cannot be achieved through insulation against others upon whom we are dependent; a child cannot discover who he is by severing his relationships with his parents; a White man cannot discover his true identity in the United States if he insulates himself against contacts with Negroes, for his own being is inseparable from theirs; personal identity emerges in dialogue with those to whom our lives are bound by common humanity and interdependence.[31]

The churches can only embody or mediate a true identity to their members when the fellowship of members represents the interdependencies of human life. Inclusiveness is intrinsic and not accidental to the nature of the Church. This crucial problem confronts all churches in the modern metropolis; the residential neighborhood of the metropolis, sundered from the community of work, undermines any representation of the interdependent society. Association by likeness rules in the residential neighborhood and informs the life of the congregation; thus, the congregational fellowship ceases to be the reconciling encounter of differences and becomes a crystallization of estrangement. The local congregation becomes the instrument of middle-class conformity rather than the reconciling force between blue collar and white collar, Negro and White. Released by the Gospel from the enslaving conformities of class, color, external appearance, and social approval, the churches exemplify the iron law of conformity which now dominates middle-class life. In fact, this iron law of conformity so dominates the life of the congregation that the truly devout are forced to seek religious nurture outside the churches; meanwhile, the central cities become increasingly the scene of blight and disorder. When communal interdependence is denied in human association, whether in forms of apartheid or economic bondage, every encounter between different groups precipitates conflict. The aggravation of such conflicts is already widespread in South Africa and is endemic to the large cities of the United States.[32] The denial of interdependence leads to destructive conflict because interdependence is the essence of humanity and men rebel at the denial of their humanity.

The problem of Protestantism in the metropolis begins to emerge more clearly from this consideration of its fellowship and mission. The prosperity of the major denominations has come from identification with the struggle of the middle classes to find security on the economic ladder. Since the economic ladder is the ladder to heaven for most Americans, the churches prosper—not so much because they are a means of ascent as stabilizing points en route. The major denominations have made no real gains in membership beyond population growth during the last twenty years; yet, they continued to expand their local building programs. The nominal members are willing to contribute to buildings that will ennoble their local communities; they are much less willing to contribute to benevolences for others or to provide ministries in remote places. The explosion in denominational construction has found ready support in the middle-class ranks so long as the proposed building was limited to their own community. Such buildings are monuments to middle-class consumption. The churches are identified with consuming communities in a society which segregates consuming from producing communities. The net effect is a cult of consumption rather than mission and ministry.

The building explosion also means exclusion from the central city and confinement to the iron cage of middle-class conformity. The Protestant minister easily becomes the number-one victim of middle-class conformity. He feels his exclusion from the producing world and missionary task principally as an enslavement to suburban children and the hypochondria which now characterizes the middle classes. He becomes a supplement to the didie service. His scholarship, preaching, teaching, and even devotion are soon drained off into the great blob of middle-class culture, a culture which subordinates the depth and meaning of religious life to the middle-class preoccupation with children.

The tragedy of this present state of most, though not all, denominational churches is the fact that many middle-class people come to church in search of the ultimate meaning of life; they, too, feel trapped with the children and the conformity. However trivial middle-class religious life may seem, the fundamental thrust is a desperate search for meaning, fullness, purpose, true identity, and freedom from conformist enslavement. This authentic aspect of the middle-class religious interest is being "sold short" by the religious life of the major denominations. Middle-class culture is a smothering blanket to its creators, for they, too, are victims. How completely the denominations are missing the real point of this search becomes evident when we consider the style of association that now dominates Protestant religious activity. The cultus of the Church has given way to the manipulations of the organization. In place of the sacraments, we have the committee meeting; in place of confession, the bazaar; in place of pilgrimage, the dull drive to hear the deadly speaker; in place of community, a collection of functions. This trivialization of religious life has made the middle-class search for religious meaning even more desperate. One begins to wonder after a time whether the search itself isn't pointless, since every church activity seems to lead further into a maze of superficiality which is stultifying the middle-class community.

FOUR: **The New Religious Style**

The separation of residence from place of work has given an artificial, almost hothouse character to the middle-class neighborhood. The church is one of the plants that grows profusely in this hothouse atmosphere. Religious fellowship becomes association by likeness; furthermore, the mission of the church becomes co-optation. The residential area used to be the point of intersection of complex forces—economic, political, communal, recreational, and familial. The residential area is now a private sphere in which families try to achieve emotional stability and to secure their position on the ladder of achievement.

The bondage of churches to the residential enclave tells only part of the story of Protestantism in the metropolis. The inner life of churches has also changed through identification with the new role of residential community. Change is endemic to a society committed to increasing its control of the physical environment. Most human societies have cherished stability and tradition; changes came slowly and furtively through the interstices of such societies. Commitment to old ways—the conservative in man's nature—suffers radical disruption in a productive society. Old ways become synonymous with inefficient, inadequate, and even erroneous procedures. "Old" becomes a pejorative term except when applied to the refined activities of the antique hunter. Residential areas likewise suffer from the disruptive forces of a productive society. Neighborhoods change character with every generation; the very idea of a homestead loses significance. The stabilities of residential life become the momentary stability of a single generation which sees its neighborhood disrupted before the children are grown. Residential community plays a new role in the society as it is sundered from the producing community; it also becomes the scene of changes which many societies have never known. The changes in the texture of residential community are reflected in the new style of religious life. The transient, shifting population of the metropolitan neighborhood dissolves the "natural," organic ties between people. The basis of congregational integrity dissolves; in fact, the human materials of friendship and familial ties are no longer available. The churches try to create fellowships without any common base in long-standing association and familiarity. The only common elements among residents of the new type of neighborhood are a relatively similar position on the economic ladder and some similarity in style of life. Where these common elements are missing, as they are in most of the inner city areas, the congregation simply dwindles and dies or develops some special field of interest. Where the common elements are present, a new style of religious life emerges—the organization church.

The term "organization" is rooted in the notion of the organic. It refers to the interdependence of elements through which structure is sustained. Hence, we refer to organs of the body as substructures and of the body as an organism. In America, organization is a word with unhappy connotations, since it implies central administration, bureaucratic structure, and political domination. These are usually considered undesirable features by Americans; in fact, it is axiomatic to American social philosophy that action originating from the individual is good, and action originating from government or a large organization is evil. There is no particular virtue in individual rather than corporate initiative, since the goodness or badness of an action cannot be defined simply by its source. The uneasiness about corporate action in the United States stems, of course, from fear of concentrated power, a fear that has led to a general prejudice against organization as such.[1] Our consideration of the organization church attempts to avoid this prejudice. The organization church creates problems in the ministry to metropolitan areas, but the problems arise from limits in the purposes and extent of organization rather than in organization as such.

It will help our analysis of the churches if the term "organization" is understood. An organization is a formal ordering of activities for the accomplishment of some purpose. There are varying degrees of formality in organizations: large industrial organizations have elaborate tables of organization with carefully specified descriptions of activities; local charities and religious groups are usually somewhat less formal. Organization can be useful, since it expedites work and co-ordinates tasks in a line of command. Organization can also be a problem, since it co-ordinates and directs activities of persons whose humanity is inseparable from freedom.

In America religious congregations have not been elaborately organized until recent years; a women's group, a Sunday school, the worship service, and an occasional fellowship meal comprised the organized activities of most early rural churches. The simple organization of the rural congregation changed under urban conditions, since urban life itself created new problems. However, the elaboration of organization reflects much deeper changes in the nature of the congregation. A type of congregation has emerged whose essential character is intimately bound up with its organizational style.

We take the highly organized congregation for granted today; moreover, we still call it a parish or congregation according to the particular denominational tradition under consideration. Nevertheless, the organization church is not a congregation, as the word is understood in the Reformation tradition; it is not even a parish in the usual meaning of the term. The organization church is a new style which emerged under urban conditions. To understand Protestantism in the metropolis, it is essential to grasp the nature of this new religious style and the reasons for its development.

NEW ACTIVITIES AND MINISTRIES

The metropolitan church is a complex maze of activities, groups, and committees; in fact, new missions often start with auxiliaries and committees. Long before a church building is constructed, subsidiary organizations have begun their various projects. In this respect, churches are similar to many other associations in American life. It is not uncommon to find three or four hundred organizations functioning in small cities of the United States. William Lloyd Warner's research team identified 899 groups and organizations in Yankee City.[2] In general, the churches reflect an American style of life in their organizational elaboration. They have also developed a viable form of association for a highly mobile society.

Scout troops, clubs, bands, young people's fellowships, and other activities organized by age and sex have developed in an urban setting. Precisely when these groups emerged is not clear. When social research on religious life began in the 1920s, however, the elaboration of activities had already occurred.[3] By 1920 urban churches were markedly different from rural churches in organizational development; in fact, H. Paul Douglass and his associates repeatedly noted this distinguishing mark of the urban church in the course of their research.[4] It was not urbanism, however, that led to the emergence of the organizational style of religious life. This style spread wherever organic or natural communities were dissolved; consequently, the organizational style has spread rapidly in rural areas in recent years. Today, the organizational style is the accepted pattern in denominational churches, since the communal fabric has been weakened in most of the areas where such churches flourish. The external mark of the organization church is the bustle of activities which are only indirectly connected with the sacred aspects of religious life.

Nurture groups and interest groups for children and young people supplemented the Sunday school; these were recreational groups with some emphasis on religious training. They represented a unique religious development. The scout troop, for example, is a training group for personal character and morals which usually plays down explicitly religious teaching. This has also been true of most other young people's groups in the churches. The churches moved outside the bounds of specifically religious training when they launched their programs of activities. Although such activities come under the broad heading of religious nurture, they are directed to the development of social and recreational interests rather than to specifically religious instruction.

In addition to the nurture groups, urban churches developed a number of organizations for adults; men's clubs, couples' clubs, old age clubs, and women's auxiliaries became popular.[5] Women's groups usually combine projects of social service and church support with sociability. Men's groups generally concentrate on fund-raising and recreational interests. While these organizations afford a certain amount of instruction, they are primarily the means for providing opportunities for association among members of the congregation; the network of organizational association extends even beyond the immediate membership of the congregation, for activities and organizations offer a semireligious atmosphere for outsiders to participate in congregational life. Interest groups for boys and girls likewise broaden the base of participation by attracting young people whose parents are not members of the congregation.

Some large urban churches have developed special ministries and activities for the welfare of underprivileged groups in the neighborhood. This type of social welfare emerged in special settings and has never become typical of urban churches; for example, after World War I, roughly 4 per cent of urban churches were engaged in this type of program.[6] These churches attempted to minister to the special needs of people in areas of social disorganization. They carried a dual program, since the ministry to the disorganized area seldom recruited adults to the congregation; furthermore, these churches represent a special case in Protestant development, for they institutionalize social and religious concern for the territory surrounding their church buildings, yet they sustain separate programs for their own congregations. Although they minister to dual and triple constituencies, they rarely bring these constituencies into a common life.

In addition to nurture groups and adult activities, the urban church has developed a complex pattern of government by committees. Members are recruited to committee work for fund-raising, building maintenance, special projects, and planning. In one city church more than seventy committees were recently at work on a major fund-raising project. Administration by committee fits the democratic pattern of Protestant organization; in fact, Protestantism has always vested considerable responsibility in the decision-making power of lay groups, but the co-ordination of events for various groups on a church calendar accentuated this aspect of Protestant life. Allocation of facilities to various activities and the orderly planning of events cannot be left to the chance decisions of innumerable groups; one large church near Chicago, for example, attracts thousands of people to its parish facilities every week; planning such a complex round of activities is a large undertaking in a democratic group. The urban church has effected co-ordination of activities through a council of committees; the full picture of organizational elaboration, therefore, must include the echelons of committees which have developed around co-ordination and planning.

The urban church is a network of interdependent activities and administrative units. It is, in short, an organization, if by organization one means the formal ordering of activities toward some goal. The goal is not sharply defined in the churches; although the organization church is broadly directed to the religious task, much of its activity is not specifically sacred.

The organization church has continued to develop as the basic type of religious association in urban life, and since the 1920s the rural churches have also adopted this pattern.[7] A crucial indication of the development of the organization church is the amount of time spent by the ordained ministry on administrative work: ministers in slightly organized urban churches in the 1920s were spending almost one fourth of their time on administration.[8] As churches become more complexly organized, time devoted to administration increases considerably; a recent study of rural churches disclosed that ministers were spending 37 per cent of their time on administrative work.[9] This finding would suggest that the organization church is now a general style in denominational churches; moreover, pastors of metropolitan churches of the major denominations today spend close to one half of their time on various types of administration.

The emergence of the organization church has transformed the practice of the ordained ministry. The ordained minister today is far more a director than a preacher or priest. H. Richard Niebuhr in a recent study of the training required for the ministry described the contemporary minister as a "pastoral director" and suggested that the new minister may emerge as a "democratic pastoral administrator, that is to say, one responsible for holding in balance, invigorating, and maintaining communication among a host of activities and their responsible leaders, all directed toward a common end."[10] It is an apt description of the organizational pastor.

The growth of administrative responsibility has been accompanied by the development of large staffs of ministers who specialize in various tasks; in fact, complexity of program and development of staff go hand in hand with the emergence of the organization church.[11] Ordained ministers are still preachers, priests, teachers, and pastors; these traditional tasks, however, are now fused into the principal task of maintaining and co-ordinating the organizational life of the congregation or parish. To meet the diverse needs of such an elaborate organization, special ministries to children, youth, adults, and nonmembers have been developed. A single pastor or priest cannot cope with the demands on his time and energy that have followed the development of the organization church. The minister in the organizational style has been well named the "pastoral director."

THE CONGREGATION IN A MOBILE SOCIETY

The organization church developed, according to the present interpretation, as an attempt to maintain a community of religious identity in the midst of residential mobility. In a relatively static situation, a congregation or parish can represent the religious interests of a local community, even though many of the members do not worship with the congregation; in fact, the congregation and the parish originated in the stable network of communal ties in local areas. A changing community presents quite a different problem; people come and go, memberships change, the residential community is in constant flux. In a large urban parish, where a secretary may be engaged full time merely to maintain records of membership, the idea of *representing* a local community is meaningless.

Residential mobility in the metropolis varies considerably; present estimates indicate that one person in five changes his residence every year.[12] In discussing residential mobility, Peter Rossi notes that "three quarters of our urban citizens were living in 1950 in places in which they did not reside in 1940."[13] Mr. Rossi worked with two areas of rather high mobility and two relatively stable areas. In the stable areas, 14 to 16 per cent of the households had been resident in the areas for less than 23 months. In the less stable areas, 30 to 41 per cent had been in the area less than 23 months.[14] When movement of one out of every six or seven households within two years seems relatively stable, mobility has become the accepted order of the day. The cumulative effect of such mobility on metropolitan neighborhoods is considerable. When H. Paul Douglass undertook a study of religious life in Pittsburgh, he found that 41 per cent of the metropolitan population had changed residence between 1940 and 1947, an enormous turnover of residents in less than a decade.

In his study of residential mobility, Peter Rossi found that areas of high mobility showed disruption of neighborly relationships; this is particularly true for areas on a lower socio-economic level. Residents in mobile areas feel that the neighobrhood is unfriendly, that other people are unlike them in social class, even though objectively this may not be the case at all. Sociability is far lower in relatively mobile areas; in general, the intercourse which creates a social fabric of neighborhood is almost obliterated by high residential mobility.[15]

Changes in a residential community mean that congregations lose old members and gain new ones. Protestant churches have experienced very high rates of membership turnover under urban conditions; studies generally indicate that seven or more members are lost for every ten gained.[16] Because these studies of turnover have been concerned with losses and gains, they do not provide information on the tenure of all members; however, even if one assumes a continuing nucleus of membership, it is evident that annual gains and losses will create instability in a parish. Apartment house areas are an extreme example of this problem of mobility, although they are usually areas on a higher socio-economic level than mobile areas of the inner city; it is estimated that churches experience a turnover of one fourth to one third of their membership every year in apartment house areas.[17] The congregation as a community of persons is obviously under extreme handicaps when memberships change so rapidly.

The organization church is well designed to cope with a changing constituency. The significance of this fact becomes somewhat clearer when the problems of a religious congregation in an area of high residential mobility are contrasted with those of other kinds of organizations. Peter Rossi has suggested two broad types of organization which face different problems of adjustment in areas of high mobility. The *client-oriented* type of organization operates by maintaining relationships between personnel and clients; a retail store is a typical example. Residential mobility creates problems for this type of organization, especially when the social or racial character of a neighborhood changes; these changes, however, can be handled by the organization through staff changes and, where necessary, through changes in the quality of merchandise.[18] The *member-oriented* type of organization depends upon relationships between members as well as between staff and clients; a boy scout program, for example, develops through relationships with staff but also through relationships between the boys in the troop; the morale of such organizations requires stable relations between members. Member-oriented organizations suffer much more radically from high residential mobility; they also have greater difficulty in dealing with changes in the composition of local populations.

Protestant churches tend to be member-oriented organizations, for they place considerable weight upon relationships among members; this emphasis was, in fact, a basic aspect of the shift from ecclesiastical institution to congregational community during the Reformation.[19] The significance of the congregation in Protestantism rests on the conviction that the priesthood is embodied in a community of believers and not solely in a priestly office. The Roman Catholic type of organization, by contrast, tends to be client-oriented. Community among members may be valuable, desirable, and even important in the Roman Catholic parish, but the parish realizes its principal religious activities through the mediation of the priest.

The client-oriented character of Roman Catholic organization has given it a certain flexibility in areas of high residential mobility. In fact, Roman Catholic parishes have usually dealt with changes in local populations through changes in staff. This does not mean that the pastors of the Roman Catholic parishes have not desired more stable communities and more adequate relationships between members; the system of fixed geographical parishes, however, has placed considerable weight upon the client-oriented aspects of Roman Catholic organization; people come and go, but the parishes remain relatively fixed. Perhaps it is this fixity of parish location which creates the client-oriented stress that Joseph Fichter describes by suggesting that many parishioners use the parish much like a "service station."[20]

The more liturgical churches of Protestantism fall somewhere between the client-oriented approach of Roman Catholicism and the more extreme member-orientation of the congregational type. The Protestant Episcopal Church would be a case in point. The Protestant Episcopal Church has maintained its geographical parishes with fair consistency in urban areas; its church buildings are rarely sold, since the property is under the control of the bishops. Nevertheless, congregational life has played a much larger part in the Protestant Episcopal form than it has in Roman Catholicism; consequently, changes in staff could not always be made expeditiously in order to meet changes in local population; moreover, the sacramental emphasis has rarely been sufficiently dominant to sustain memberships despite decline of local community relationships. The net effect has been a relatively static parish system in the Protestant Episcopal Church with great losses of membership in inner city areas; in general, even the more liturgical Protestant churches have moved in the direction of the organization church in order to meet problems of urban mobility. Joseph Fichter notes considerable organizational development in Roman Catholic parishes, which would suggest that organizational activities create a certain degree of relationship between members even in the client-oriented type of churches. Perhaps no religious association can completely approach the impersonality of the client-oriented organization exemplified by the chain store.

Protestant congregations have attempted to sustain relationships between members despite residential mobility and turnover of membership. They have accomplished this in two ways: (1) they have drawn the members into innumerable organizational activities; (2) they have stressed the pastoral relationship to the clergy. The organizational program has served to create organizational interdependence among members. The client relationship to the clergy has provided a feeling of personal membership. This combination of organizational activity and personal loyalty to the minister weaves the fabric of the organization church, which is a substitute for residential community.

Two types of congregational activity create a network of relationships between members: activities of subsidiary organizations and the work of committees for special projects. For present purposes, nurture groups can be dropped from consideration, since they are largely training groups for younger members of the congregation. These groups are important for developing loyalty to the church in a changing population; moreover, they provide opportunities for service and learning. Their significance, however, will be considered in another context.

The organizational activities contribute to the maintenance of the congregation. Choirs provide music; women's groups sponsor fund raising and social services; men's groups provide recreation and fund-raising projects. The organizing goal of most of these activities, in addition to providing attractive interest groups for the potential members, is the maintenance of the congregation as a going concern. The social service aspect of some of the activity tends to be secondary, although money is raised in this way for various kinds of benevolence. The committees contribute directly to the maintenance of congregational life; in general, committee activities create channels for participation in the work of the organization. The organization church seeks its own preservation, emerges when the natural basis of community is weakened by mobility, and strengthens the fabric of membership through organizational participation.

Common activity toward a common goal develops unity and

loyalty in a group; this is as true in neighborhood organization as it is in a church; in fact, when people participate in the work of an organization, they feel that they belong. Clergymen often say that if a new member is given a job, he will become a loyal member. Whether he ushers, cooks, raises funds, or recruits members, he contributes to the support of the organization and has a stake in its success. Even these essentially impersonal performances on behalf of the common goal generate loyalty to the organization and a consensus about the value of the local church. The organization, in other words, creates a network of interdependent activities and functions through which members develop loyalties to the organization. Members who have helped to build up a congregation and even construct its building will often speak longingly of the good old days when there was real spirit in the congregation.

Minimizing personal ties is essential to organizations in areas of high residential mobility. It is not necessary to know another person intimately in order to co-operate on a bazaar or fund-raising project; in fact, such activities help to break the ice between strangers. The emphasis in the organization church is upon contributions to the organization; if a new member can sing, he or she will be invited to join the choir; if a man is skilled in carpentry, he will be recruited for the committee on maintenance. The organization church does not require intimate relationships among members to substain its internal life.

The impersonality of the organization church can easily be exaggerated; participation in a women's guild is after all one way to meet other women. Nevertheless, one can make friends or not in these organizations and still participate; in this sense the organization church is independent of the network of friendships in the outside community from which the members are recruited. This is one of its great strengths. If the outside community lacks any semblance of common life, the congregation can help to fill the void through its organizational activities.

Independence of the surrounding community is the distinguishing mark of the organization church. Organizational activity creates a network of relationships independent of the unstable social fabric of the metropolis. This is a radical transformation in the nature and role of the congregation, which was originally a gathering of believers who represented the community and its common interests. These congregations borrowed their communal fabric from the surrounding community; the special task of the congregation was to worship, hear the Word preached, and receive the sacrament on behalf of the surrounding community. However inadequately this principle of representation may have been realized in the gathered congregation, (it is quite unnecessary to romanticize it), there was little need to fabricate a community through activity, since the congregation existed because there was a community. To greater and lesser degrees, congregational representation appeared in Puritan, pietistic, and sectarian strands of the Protestant development. The life of the surrounding community was leavened and enhanced by the witness of the believing community. To be sure, representation often became a pietistic rejection of the local community or even a legalistic suppression of the liberties of unbelieving neighbors; nevertheless, the gathered congregation was a potent religous form because it drew its internal communal strength from the network of social bonds in the social environment. The organization church appeared when this social network in the residential community was weakened, marking the end of the representative community of believers. The gathered congregation became an organization which could endure despite the dissolution of residential community and could create a sense of community in the membership. Religious congregating became independent of the local community from which its members were recruited. The organization church appeared as a substitute form of community rather than a representation of an existing community. It filled the communal void created by urban mobility, providing a vehicle for social identity of the middle classes.

Two problems arise with respect to the organization church as a form of the Christian Church: (1) there is an obvious question about the religious significance of the organizational network in the congregation; (2) there is an additional question about the loyalty created in the organization church—loyalty to what or whom? In what sense, if any, can this organizational life of the congregation be considered religiously significant? And what is its effect on the missionary concern of the churches?

THE MEANING OF THE ACTIVITY

Activities have direct and indirect effects; for example, the observable effect of fund raising is the provision of money. Organization churches, however, engage in two types of fund raising: on the one hand, committees undertake highly organized and ambitious programs—obtaining pledges, keeping accounts, planning budgets and occasionally hiring outside organizations; on the other hand, many of the subsidiary organizations also spend considerable time and energy on fund raising—conducting sales or organizing suppers, for example—time and energy that could just as well be provided through regular channels. The meaning of these fund-raising activities is puzzling. Does the subsidiary activity have significance for the members over and above the obvious purpose of providing money? Do the members find emotional satisfaction in these sacrifices of time and energy, so that arguments in favor of more rational fund raising could not discourage them from their activities? Do these activities accomplish more for the members than might be guessed from the observable effects?

W. Lloyd Warner, who has touched upon a similar question in his study of the associational activities of Yankee City, interprets the exchanges of gifts within voluntary associations and between various organizations as symbolic ways of confirming membership in a common community; the gift evokes feelings of belonging between members and groups; social class differences and other barriers are symbolically denied by the exchange of gifts and a common ground of community is created.[21]

This view of gift exchange was originally developed as an interpretation of activities in simpler societies; for example, the Potlatch among Indians of the Northwest had been interpreted as a symbolic working out of rivalries over differences in social status; thus, sentiments of solidarity are evoked and feelings of envy and malice drained off in the symbolic competition of gift giving. The exchanges in the organization church can be interpreted in a similar way as expressing solidarity and evoking deeper feelings of unity.

This type of analysis illuminates the dual form of fund raising in the organization church: (1) the rational, organized programs provide opportunities for members to express loyalty to the organization, to "pledge" themselves to the congregation (the term itself is suggestive), and yet this rational type of fund raising leaves little room for a network of exchange in which members can feel solidarity; (2) opportunities for exchange are provided in the subsidiary organizations which enlist members in a complex round of activities, as in the fellowship supper where members contribute the food, prepare the meal, pay for the tickets, and buy back the leftovers. Members who give their time, money, energy, and skill to this kind of informal fund raising are elated over the success of their ventures; the pastor congratulates one and all; the members are relieved when the burdensome duty is over, yet they feel a sense of membership in the congregational fellowship. From some perspectives, such an expense of energies seems wasted, but those who participate feel that it deepens their sense of belonging to the church. It is this symbolic aspect of the organizational network which elicits support for its endless round of "busy-ness."

There is a significant difference between primitive gift exchanges and the activities of the organization church. Primitive people are bound together in networks of primary groups; familial ties hedged in by taboos and ritualized patterns of behavior are intensely developed in their communities; thus, gift exchanges are expressions of positive and negative feelings, evoking the sentiments of mutual confidence and affection which are essential to a closely knit community. Gift exchanges between different tribes are often a means of overcoming fears of hostile action and evoking feelings of mutual trust.

Gift exchange in the organization church is much more intertribal than intratribal, since members lack close ties with one another. The only intimate group in the metropolis is the nuclear family of husband, wife, and children; therefore, members of a congregation are often unfamiliar with the names of other members; consequently, exchanges in the organization church create mutual confidence and familiarity, help members to feel that they belong, even though they are not knit into an intimate community. The activities do not resolve tensions already existing within and between groups, but they do evoke a sense of belonging to a common community. Thus, the exchanges help to fashion community feeling rather than to preserve stability against the disruptive forces of overly intimate relationships. The round of activities in the organization church is a celebration of its own unity through which some sense of community is evoked.

A puzzling feature of the organization church is the recruitment of members to do things which would be considered intolerable drudgery at home: hours of telephoning, cooking, cleaning, serving, endless correspondence. How is it possible? What light does it shed on the meaning of the activities of the organization church?

Undoubtedly, many members welcome an outlet for their energies and an opportunity to achieve status through organizational achievement; by conducting meetings and running bazaars they find recognition for their efforts. Such an interpretation may account for the preoccupation with slates of officers and programs, but it does not explain the psychic energies expended.

It is possible that organizational activities provide some members with a means to work out feelings of guilt through sacrifices of time and energy in organizational drudgery. This interpretation explains the "drive" behind much of the activity. Although members often complain about the drudgery, they not only do it but seem to need it as well. Their cherished Sunday mornings are devoted to one semireligious activity or another as a way of atoning for guilt feelings through sacrificial behavior.

The idea of atoning for guilt through organizational drudgery suggests that the activities of the churches provide a Protestant system of penance. Members do penance for their faults by sharing in the organizational work. (Penance is an obligation imposed by the church as discipline for a sin. A penitential system is a way of mediating grace or forgiveness through the performance of certain ritualized acts such as repeating psalms or prayers. The most familiar system of penance developed in the monastic life of the medieval church: confession of sins was followed by an imposition of penance, consisting of spiritual works for amendment of life; certain prayers or psalms were repeated, and, in some cases, other forms of punishment or discipline were imposed. This system of penance was gradually institutionalized in parish churches, and the penitential system became a functioning part of the sacramental system.) Cooking a supper or serving on a committee may seem far removed from repeating the Hail Mary, but organizational drudgery does seem to fulfill a similar function in the metropolitan congregation; members atone for their guilt by performing unpleasant tasks for the organization; to this extent, the organizational network becomes a secularized penitential system, and the pastor who solicits their labors becomes the punishing father.

The compulsive character of activity in religious organizations is illuminated by the notion that feelings of guilt are worked out through sacrificial action for the organization.[22] Feelings of guilt must be purged in one way or another in a sinful world; by rejecting sacramental penance, Protestantism opened the way for the development of secularized penance. There are optimal levels of guilt which can be creative, stimulating members to resolve personal and interpersonal problems. In this sense, the activities of the organization church drain off energies which could flow into creative ministries and problem solving. The organization church becomes, thus, a substitute for creative religious action, a vehicle of "cheap" grace.[23] Dietrich Bonhoeffer used the term "cheap" grace with reference to forgiveness without obligation, faith without obedience, gift without demand. In these terms the organization church mediates forgiveness by imposing trivial and irrelevant obligations which incidentally redound to the glory of the organization; thus the gift of forgiveness is burdened with drudging demands and the commandment to love thy neighbor ignored; the free gift of grace is obscured and the costly demand of the Gospel trivialized.

Two significant aspects emerge from this analysis of the organization church: (1) members have an opportunity to identify themselves with the religious organization through the network of organizational activity, experiencing feelings of loyalty as the congregation celebrates its own unity; (2) sacrifices of time and energy in the organization church offer members atonement for their feelings of guilt through an elaborate penitential system. These aspects are intimately related, of course, since sacrifices to the organization could not alleviate feelings of guilt unless the members felt strongly their identity with the organization; hence, a sense of belonging to this sacred collectivity and willingness to sacrifice to it are interdependent experiences. The significance of the organizational network is seen in the community of belonging it provides in the flux of metropolitan change, and the reconciliation it offers members confronted by their own failures and guilt feelings.

The celebration of organizational unity and the resolution of feelings of guilt through drudgery serve to create a religious unit (parish or congregation) independent of the changing population of a metropolitan community. Organizational activities make it possible to incorporate new members and lose old ones with a minimum of strain; to be sure, more stable residential areas strengthen these religious units, since membership changes create many problems; nevertheless, the virtue of the organization church is its resistance to disruption by residential mobility.

LOYALTY **AND** MISSIONARY POTENTIAL

The deeper religious forces which draw some people into religious activity and leave others outside cannot be appraised in this type of analysis. Why some people join churches and others do not has plagued theologians throughout history. Our concerns are much less profound than an answer to this question. We are asking why the organizational style makes sense in middle-class culture. It obviously has little or no appeal to working-class people, unless they aspire to middle-class life. What is the interest that draws middle-class people into this particular style of expression for their religious concerns? And what are the consequences for mission?

It should be noted that many church members avoid committees and activities. The organizational style is the dominant motif in denominational religious life, but it is far from an exclusive motif.

In a study of twelve congregational churches in an urban setting—central city, suburban, one all-Negro, one integrated—Yoshio Fukuyama found that one third of all official members are nominal members who contribute but give very little outside the congregation for benevolence and attend services only sporadically. Of the remaining two thirds, almost 50 per cent are addicted to the organizational style in an extreme degree. This means that roughly two thirds of the official membership in these churches enjoy a *cultic style* of membership (combining nominal with organizational activists). The remaining one third distribute about equally between a *devotional style* (oriented to personal prayer), an *intellectual style* (oriented to religious ideas), and a *creedal style* (oriented to traditional beliefs).[24] The dominant motif in Fukuyama's sample is identification with a worshiping and active organization or association. He calls this a cultic orientation. The minority styles have played a significant part in other periods of religious history; for example, the devotional style approaches closely the mystical type of religious orientation, emphasizing union with God and imitation of the divine life. It is evident that these minority styles have little place in the organization church; in fact, Mr. Fukuyama finds that the intellectual style is confined to those who are well educated and intellectually active, while the devotional style is limited largely to those who are isolated or elderly. The organizational style is only one of several possible types of religious orientation today, but it clearly dominates the middle-class pattern of the denominational church.

The findings from this congregational church study are illuminating with respect to the question: loyalty to what? H. Paul Douglass had studied the development of organizational membership in the suburbs of cities such as St. Louis and Springfield, Massachusetts, in the 1920s, and drew attention to the fact that churches were raveling out into an organizational network lacking seriousness with respect to worship and the more serious business of the churches. The nominal membership and the organizational activists of the congregational study represent the working out of these trends which Douglass had detected in the suburban churches. The middle-class membership pours its energies into the local organization. The nominal group holds membership and gives financial support, even though it feels little or no commitment to the religious object of the church's loyalty. Here evidently is an identification with a social collectivity—the organization church. Organizational loyalty may also explain why more than one half of a sampling of new members in Pittsburgh churches had switched denominations.[25] It seems reasonable to assume that approximately one half of the official membership of the churches, possibly as much as two thirds, are religiously tied to an organization rather than personally bound to God or his teachings—a suprising fact in view of the Protestant understanding of faith.

It is ironical that Protestantism, after rebelling against the institutional character of Roman Catholicism, should emerge in the 1960s with a membership predominantly oriented to organizational activities and concentrated in the middle years—families with growing children, high earning power, and more than average energy. In other words, Protestantism today represents the dominant group in America's productive process.

The clue to the religious significance of this organizational membership is provided by its activistic style, which emphasizes external criteria of performance as a basis of evaluation: not how you *feel* or what you *believe* but what you *do*. The good church member is one who *does* things: *works* on this, *accomplishes* that. The activism of this religious style is a clue to its real meaning. In a mobile, productive society, people feel that they belong when they perform on behalf of the collectivity—whether the performance be in occupation or church. They become functions within this collectivity and identify themselves with it. This means losing one's self-identify in the hope of discovering another identity through surrender to the collectivity.[26] It is noteworthy, in this connection, that those who are active in churches also tend to be active in community associations. They *are* because they *do*.

The search for meaning through activity and performance is typically middle class. To be a successful middle-class person is to perform adequately. To be a middle-class Christian is to perform well on the committee. Thus, the organization church is the community of good works—the new style of salvation by works which has invaded the Reformation churches. It is a typically middle-class style of association. No wonder these denominational churches fail miserably in the lower-class areas of cities unless they change their programs radically.

The interesting aspect of this style of salvation by works is that it contradicts the new theology which is informing the ministry of the post-World War II period. This new ministry has been indoctrinated with existential despair, the rediscovery of the Bible, and the recent emphasis on "last things" as the only "important things." Preaching what it considers to be Biblical orthodoxy on Sundays, during the rest of the week it rushes about to oil the organizational machinery. Six days a week it enlists laymen for activities which promise salvation through good works. On Sunday, salvation is by faith through grace. The minority of creedally oriented members are fed by the sermon on Sunday; the majority of organizational members are fed by activity through the week.

The belief in salvation through works which is conveyed in the organizational style is more than a confusion of the Message. The appeal of this style is that it solidifies the sense of belonging in a community of social identity; one feels united with a collectivity symbolizing a particular rung on the economic ladder. Here we encounter the full force of the search for social identity in residential communities. The churches become symbols of the collective identity of middle-class groups in their neighborhoods. The changing world of metropolitan society is blotted out of the picture, and the local group becomes the significant universe to which the family belongs. In this process, the sacred organization becomes the means to sanctify one's position on the economic ladder; the precarious perch gains a semblance of permanence.

One cannot answer the question of "loyalty to what?" for every member of an organization church. These loyalties range over the many problems and interests of the variegated life of the modern metropolis. We have already noted this fact in the diversity of religious styles. Nevertheless, the associational meaning of this style is fairly evident; it is assurance of personal adequacy through proper performances, even as the medieval conception of sacraments involved a mechanical mode of assuring eternal life. Moreover, the sense of middle-class identity through participation in this collectivity seems to be a significant aspect of the denominational church for a majority of its members. The collapse of the fabric of personal community in the residential areas of the metropolis aggravated the search for social identity. The organization church emerged from the crisis of social identity which came with population change, the dissolution of "natural" communities, and the expansion of the middle classes. It represents an island of conformity in the metropolis—a treadmill where men and women grind out their salvation.

The circle of activity in the organization church offers a sense of participating in a sacred reality which promises fullness in place of the emptiness of a materialistic culture. The creation of this treadmill followed the breakdown of "natural" communities and the consequent search for a significant anchorage in the flux of metropolitan life. The trivialization of the religious enterprise through the activism of this new style has to do more with the content of the activity than the fact that the style is activistic. Some people have a strong need to express themselves through doing. Certainly it is true of many middle-class people. Although the contemplative and mystical styles will probably continue to be minor notes in our culture, all groups need more opportunities for quiet reflection than are afforded by the new religious style, which is impoverishing the religious life of our culture by the triviality of so much of its action.

The enriched activity of the organization church will come only as its identification with a local, residential enclave is loosened. Many pastors and laymen have already enriched the churches by cultivating groups for nurture and fellowship among all age levels. Such ventures, and especially the development of "house churches" and neighborhood fellowships, can go a long way toward deepening the religious quality of the organization church. The key problem in the long run, however, will be to stake out an area of ministry for the congregation which includes the diversity of residential areas and peoples of the metropolis. The activity of the organization church can become mission and reconciling fellowship only as it includes the interdependent life of the metropolis. Such *inclusive* expression of the Church in contrast to the present bondage of the churches to *exclusive* residential areas is the most difficult task facing the churches in the metropolis. The forces of metropolitan life continually press familial and religious groups toward preoccupation with their own activities; then the organization church becomes a dreary treadmill and the Message is trivialized to an assurance that the emptiness of middle-class life is all that life was meant to be anyway. The net effect is for the church to become an end in itself—a collective symbol of the sanctity of middle-class values. When the church becomes a collective, it ceases to subordinate its identity to its reconciling task in the world; in fact it resists external claims for ministry and help, turning in upon itself. This introversion of the organization church is the last stage of the shackling of the major denominations to middle-class culture and the real source of the impoverishment of middle-class religion.

The introverted church is one which puts its own survival before its mission, its own identity above its task, its internal concerns before its apostolate, its rituals before its ministry. These contrasts distinguish the Church as a structure and the Church as a living power—its static and dynamic aspects. Historical embodiments of the Church tend to stress one of these aspects at the expense of the other; in recent times the introverted church stresses the Church as structure at the expense of the mission and task of the Church. The middle-class search for social identity has led to emphasis on the collective form of the Church; consequently, the Protestant congregation, one of the most dynamic forms in the history of the Church, has become a static, organizational entity. Undue emphasis on the static structure of the Church has led to the disappearance of a significant lay ministry in denominational Protestantism. Loss of dynamic form and surrender of mission undercut the lay ministry, for it is the Church as mission which rests its case upon the laity and their outreach to the world. The more introverted the Church, the more it becomes subject to priestcraft and routinized activities. The introverted church substitutes celebrations of its own unity for witness in the metropolis. An introverted church is an apostate body, for it denies the essential quality of Church—the testimony of reconciliation in the world.

The denominations refuse to take the introversion of the churches seriously. They believe it is accidental and will be overcome by building enough churches in the suburbs. They will not face the fact that they are doing the same thing today which they did at the turn of the century, and will shackle the churches even more firmly to the treadmill of the introverted congregation.

The seriousness and pervasiveness of this introversion can be seen even more vividly in the transmutation of ethnic, Negro, and sectarian churches, which have struggled to express particular religious identities amidst the corrosive forces of metropolitan life. When their "natural" communities were undermined by movement into the middle-class ranks, these bodies developed an organizational style with an accentuated introversion. This link between the new religious style, the local enclave, and the introverted church creates the inhibiting force to the mission in the metropolis. When we appreciate how closely the introversion of the church is interwoven with its tie to middle-class enclaves, we can begin to think in terms of inclusive congregations and the responsibility of the church for mission and ministry. As we might expect, the very precariousness of the ethnic, Negro, and sectarian identities in the United States has accentuated the introversion of their congregations; for our purposes, however, the instructive development is the adoption of the introverted style of the organization church as these groups became middle class.

FIVE

The Introversion of the Churches

The new style of Protestantism emerged during the past century through barely perceptible changes in social and religious life. These changes created a threefold transformation in the churches: (1) an exodus to the suburbs, (2) the identification of Protestantism with the new middle class, and (3) the adoption of an organizational style of religious community in place of the representative congregation.

Several religious groups provide examples of the emergence of the new style with the breakdown of local communities. These groups were observed during the 1920s and 1930s when they were in process of transition; at different points, each of these groups gave birth to a new style of congregation; these religious changes, furthermore, were associated with the emergence of middle-class life. The changes in ethnic, Negro, and sectarian congregations provide instances of the emergence of the collective form of religious organization—the introverted church; they also give a picture of the major denominations in process of emergence.

Ethnic, Negro, and sectarian forms of religious life are obviously very different. Anyone familiar with these movements will be more sensitive to their differences than their similarities. Subsequent discussion of these styles will take cognizance of the differences, for each of these styles has its distinctive place within the total life of Protestantism; in fact, each persists to this day in metropolitan areas. There are similarities in these religious styles, however, when they are considered in relation to the new style of congregational life, similarities that can be stressed without violating the authenticity of each style. In this spirit the subsequent analysis is undertaken.

THE ETHNIC CHURCHES

Churches of the foreign-born are a familiar religious form in the United States. Although the ethnic church is passing out of existence now that immigration has been restricted, the spread of the ethnic church was one of the remarkable missionary ventures of recent centuries. It was the more remarkable because it was a spontaneous growth of a new religious form. Of course, most of the major denominations in America were originally churches of the foreign-born; the Puritan congregations of New England were as much ethnic churches as the Lithuanian and Slovak churches of later immigration; it was Anglo-Saxon prejudices that restricted the word "ethnic" to non-English-speaking communities and congregations. The spread of foreign-language churches during the great immigrations was an instance of religious colonization that has probably never been duplicated. This spontaneous growth of ethnic religious activity colonized the United States with Roman Catholic, Protestant, and Jewish congregations of the foreign-born.[1]

Protestant congregations of the foreign-born followed the older styles of Protestantism for the first generation or two; they did not assume the style of the organization church.[2] Worship, preaching, religious instruction, and traditional rites comprised the scope of activities of these ethnic congregations.

It was customary some years ago to attribute the lack of organizational development in ethnic churches to traditionalism; the idea was that the foreign-born adhered to old-country ways, refusing to adapt their religious activities to the new situation. When the idea of traditionalism is used in this way, it implies a disparagement of the nonprogressive tendencies among particular peoples; it is a value judgment about these people rather than an interpretation of their religious practices. The immigrant was anything but traditional in many things which he did; emigration from one's native soil is hardly a traditional activity. Immigrant people retained certain customs and dropped others; they were highly selective in their traditionalism; for example, some ethnic churches sponsored classes in economics; this would have seemed bizarre in the old country. An understanding of the ethnic churches must move beyond glib terms and consider the total process of Americanization through which the immigrants were passing.[3]

The basic fact about immigrant life was its discontinuity with life in the old country: many immigrants longed to escape from the poverty of the old life, its drudgery and hunger; some fled family domination or unhappy marriages; others sought easy success. Whatever the impulses that stirred particular individuals to emigrate, the actuality of broken ties was more of a shock than most of them anticipated.

Many an immigrant met difficulties and disillusionment in the New World. He was crowded into a slum, haunted by poverty, intimidated by a strange language; he knew the hopelessness of unemployment and the difficulties of adopting new ways; he aspired to a new life in the United States, but he yearned for the familiar routines of the old. The ethnic community provided security and order in the midst of these changes: the old language was spoken; familiar foods were prepared; tales from home were told and retold. The ethnic community was an island of the familiar in the midst of the alien; it lived the familiar idiom. Here the immigrant was safe, though impoverished; here he could assume a new life gradually, since the strains of new encounters were balanced by the reassurance of old ways. The ethnic community offered social continuity amidst the discontinuities of immigrant life.[4]

The immigrant anchored his life in the ethnic community: he read its papers, took his cues from older residents, and learned American politics from the professional ethnics whose life was spent in mediating between their own people and the new milieu. Ethnic organizations preserved the customary feasts; the ethnic community was, in the fullest sense, a community of social identity for the immigrant—a community in which his inner self-confidence was bolstered by the familiar responses of those of similar background. The immigrant entered the New World in the company of his own people; thus he knew who he was because this community assured him of his identity. On the street and in the loft he might forget his identity or feel like a mere tool, but the initial shock of employment in the New World was softened so long as the ethnic community offered acceptance and membership.

Ethnic religious activity can best be understood as an aspect of the total life of the ethnic community. The ethnic church contributed to the continuity of immigrant life more readily than other groups in the ethnic world, for the church preserved the foreign language which had to be replaced by English in the contacts of work and community; moreover, the church celebrated the occasions of birth, marriage, and death. Membership in the ethnic congregation sustained a sense of continuity with the old without denying orientation to the new. The ethnic church was not the state or provincial church of the old country; it was a new, American church which could at the same time fully identify itself with the life of the ethnic community. The sacred rituals and proclamation poured old meanings into the new life of the immigrant and gave a sense of order amidst the disorder of new adjustments.

. . . For some now religion became the focal point of their affiliation. Men were not drawn back to the churches by the attractiveness of theological doctrine, however; the trend toward secularism was not reversed. . . . But the most powerful magnet was the round of practices and social connections capable of giving order to life in American society. . . .[5]

The ethnic congregation was free to develop such activities as were needed in this new situation; in this sense, it was not a traditional form. This was not the congregation of the Old World, however much it may have preserved certain older forms; to be sure, general similarities in the life situation of all immigrants led to uniformities in the pattern of ethnic religious activity; for the most part, these congregations carried the burden of sacred symbolism within the total life of the ethnic community. Ethnic churches seldom engaged in recreational activities, because such interests were served through the associational groups of the immigrant community. The congregations developed few special interest groups because the ethnic community provided innumerable outlets for such interests. The ethnic church was burdened principally with the task of sacred proclamation and ritual; in most instances, it fulfilled this task with remarkable success.

The congregations of Southern and Eastern Europeans developed specialized groups for language study and other activities which were needed for adjustment to American life. In attempting to categorize these churches, H. Paul Douglass called them "widely variant" by the standards of the congregational life of the major denominations.[6] This is an apt term, for these ethnic congregations varied considerably in the style of their religious activities. The needs of later immigrants were different; their ethnic communities were weaker and less stable; they provided less in the way of intimate association and political identity. The churches bore additional burdens in these particular communities; in fact, they engaged quite freely in those activities which were crucial to the order and continuity of life in the New World.

The freedom and flexibility of the ethnic church is often overlooked, because the ethnic congregation seemed conservative to the native-born. The conservatism or adaptability of the ethnic church has little to do with traditional ties to the old country; these ties were tenuous, if they existed at all. The clue to the combination of conservatism and flexibility in ethnic religious activities is to be found rather in the ties between the ethnic church and the ethnic community. The ethnic church was religiously conservative because it carried the burden of sacred symbolism for an ethnic community; it was responsible to this community; moreover, this communal base gave the ethnic church of the first generation freedom to cling scrupulously to the old ways or venture into new styles of religious expression.[7]

The ethnic community met increasing difficulty in maintaining solidarity among the second and third generations in the New World; second-generation children may have been born in the Old World, but their schooling and childhood drew them into American ways. The conflicting attitudes of the second generation toward their foreign-born parents have furnished a familiar theme in American literature; affection for the parents and yearning for full American identity made this a generation in conflict. The children were the fulfillment of their parents' dreams of a new life; yet the parents reminded the children of their foreign origin, raising questions about their American identity. The parents were proud of the new ways which their children were assuming, yet resented the barriers which these new ways created between them and their children. These and other strains tore at the solidarity of the ethnic community, weakening the ties which held the new generation to the ethnic church.

The foreign-born community also lost its solidarity through the upward social mobility of its members. Individual families moved out of the orbit of the ethnic community as they made their way up the economic ladder; in fact, whole segments of ethnic communities began to move to better residential areas. The upwardly mobile ethnics changed the locations of their congregations and adopted the style of the organization church. Since ethnic churches were not missionary churches to the native-born populations, they avoided general recruitment in the surrounding community; hence they developed activities for the ethnic memberships and attempted to hold the second and third generations. The organizational style of the ethnic church emerged in an effort to sustain the internal life of the constituency.[8]

Two aspects of the ethnic situation illumine our understanding of the emergence of the organization church: the organizational style emerged in the second and third generations when the ethnic community no longer provided a solid base for social identity; furthermore, the organizational style developed as the children of the foreign-born moved into the middle class. In general, the weakening of the communal base of the ethnic congregation through Americanization and the upward social mobility of the people created a crisis of social identity among the immigrants. This crisis of social identity led to defections from the churches; however, the ethnic churches developed an organizational style which offered a substitute vehicle of social identity to replace the ethnic community; in fact, the organizational style emerged when the "natural" ethnic community had ceased to shape the lives of descendants of the foreign-born.

The ethnic church with an organizational style had a dual appeal for upwardly mobile ethnics. For one thing, ethnic congregations of the new style still had an ethnic coloration; the old language may have been discarded, and the style of the church was similar to congregations of the major denominations of native-born; nevertheless, the hymns, ministry, rituals, and ethnic names were familiar; thus, love and loyalty to one's parents could be expressed by identification with this congregation, for it was ethnic enough to represent the values that had shaped their lives. A second aspect of the appeal of the new style of ethnic congregation was its very similarity to the churches of the native-born; the ethnic church of the new style observed ethnic customs in food and music, but the ethnic organization church was an Americanized substitute for the congregation of the old ethnic community; to be sure, marriages and associations were kept within the orbit of the ethnic community, but this in-group now reflected an Americanized ethnicity.

The ethnic church became the basis for ethnic social identity.[9] In order to fulfill this new role for children of the foreign-born, it had to maintain acceptable ethnic traits and yet display signs of full Americanization. The organizational style met both of these requirements. It stimulated a sense of belonging without deep ethnic commitment; it reflected the style of American middle-class association in appropriate ethnic garb.

Many ethnic churches resisted the transition to the organizational style; ethnic religious life in these instances became a counterforce to the upward mobility and Americanization of immigrant children. Parents and pastors clung to an ethnic style of religion as a protest against the break-up of the ethnic community of identity; in fact, the instability of the ethnic community led to religious conservatism even as a stable ethnic base had supported flexibility in religious styles. The ethnic community still appealed to the Americanized children so long as the ethnic garb was decorative rather than essential. Community of ethnic identity had sustained the parents, but it would never again be the center of life for the third generation. This conflict between the first- and third-generation attitudes toward ethnicity reveals the transitional character of the ethnic community of identity. Ethnicity was seldom a real alternative to American identity; it was rather a mode of transition to full American identity. Ethnic communities and churches were transitional forms of identity and religious expression; in fact, when they lost their transitional, forward-looking quality and became pockets of backward-looking ethnicity, they lost their hold on the new generations and created deep conflicts in the hearts of the children. The transition from the ethnic congregation to the organizational style of middle-class church was a natural development once the ethnic community of identity had served its purpose; for, at this stage, the organization church emerged as a substitute community of social identity—the collective form of the organization church replaced the ethnic community as a focus of social identity. Ethnic introversion was replaced by the introverted church.

THE NEGRO CHURCHES

Negro churches were identified with the struggle of the Negro people from the earliest days; they were also a vehicle for the development of Negro leadership. The separation of White and Negro denominations eventuated ultimately from White discrimination, but within a tradition of social apartheid the churches were important in developing Negro leadership. Both Negro churches and educational institutions were closely interwoven with the destiny of the Negro people in the United States.[10]

The identification between Negro churches and the Negro community continued in the urban setting. Negro religious styles are better understood from this link to the Negro community than from the rural background in which this religious loyalty was nurtured. The Negro community is unique in metropolitan areas, for most Negroes have had little choice about identifying with the destiny of their people; in fact, the Negro community is a product of White discrimination, even as the Negro's need for familiar and safe association with other Negroes is the product of discrimination.[11] White people commonly say that Negroes want their own churches and desire housing among their own people; however, since White people have forced Negroes to search for Negro communities of identity, it is impossible for them to know what Negroes want; in fact, it is difficult for Negroes to know who they are or what they want. When choice is restricted for generations, it is difficult to know what choices would be made if they were possible.

The "sit-in" strikes of 1960 were an historic event in the Negro struggle because they were open expressions of the Negro's aspiration for full citizenship. The fundamental fact about the Negro community is its involuntary character—its lack of choice until recent years; this character is crucial to the role of the Negro churches.

The dynamics of the Negro community of identity correspond to its involuntary nature. Negroes are ambivalent about this community; that is, the Negro identifies himself with this community because he sees himself as Negro in his relationships with Whites; the identity, however, is one of second-class citizenship created and perpetuated by Whites; consequently, the Negro rejects his community even as he accepts it.[12] The Negro is an American citizen in every respect except in freedom to participate in the opportunities of American life. American-born, he knows only American culture. American dreams fill his imagination; American hopes weave the fabric of his future; consequently, surrendering to an imposed Negro identity is rejection of American citizenship. On the other hand, the Negro feels safer within the Negro community where he escapes discriminations on the basis of color. The Negro rejects the Negro community and his Negro identity because it symbolizes his exclusion from his birthright as an American; on the other hand, he seeks identification within the Negro community as an escape from conflict. Internally torn by the attractive security it affords and the deprivation of full citizenship which it embodies, the Negro community as a comunity of social identity is an imposed alternative to full American citizenship.[13]

The full force of the ambivalence of Negro identity was not so evident in the Negro ghettos of the 1920s and 1930s. The Negro newcomer arrived in the large city and was confined to the worst kind of slums.[14] The only work open to him was of the most menial type; no work was too hard for him, no pay too low.[15] His recreation and personal associations were confined to members of his own race in facilities provided by his community. Segregated housing meant that his children attended public school with other Negro children. He saw foreign-born workers promoted and knew that his job ceiling approached zero. Negro opportunity was so limited in the earlier period of urbanization that ambivalence was submerged in resignation to an unalterable fate; the very possibility of full citizenship had been denied in the caste system of the South and seemed to be denied again by the actuality of life in the metropolis; overcrowding, poverty, unemployment, and degradation followed the heavy in-migration of Negroes to urban areas.

The Negro congregations of the 1920s reflected the atmosphere of the Negro ghetto.[16] The preaching and hymns expressed the otherworldly hope which had characterized Negro religious life from the earliest days. Feelings released in worship gave an outlet for pent-up emotions. The lack of educational opportunities for Negroes was reflected in the ministry, which ranged from a high standard of excellence to jackleg demagoguery.[17] Negro religious life was principally an expression of the folk religiousness of the Negro community.

There was little organizational elaboration in the congregational life of Negro churches in this period; in fact, the main social group in these congregations was the informal club. Most congregations had as many as six of these clubs which met in private homes; for the most part they carried on educational, financial, and social activities on behalf of the churches. This pattern of informal organization undoubtedly reflected the lack of adequate religious facilities in the churches; these clubs provided alternative outlets, however, for association in a community excluded from the recreational opportunities of the larger community.[18] The exclusion of Negroes from metropolitan opportunities was enforced by discriminatory action, but it was also effected by economic deprivation. The Negro churches seem to have filled this void in recreational outlets by an informal pattern of religious and social activity. H. Paul Douglass classified these Negro churches as "widely variant" because their organizational style diverged sharply from that of the major denominations. The style of the Negro churches was neither traditional nor middle class; it was a style peculiarly fitted to the character and needs of the Negro community.[19]

The ambivalence within the Negro community deepened with the rise of the Negro middle class, or, in E. Franklin Frazier's graphic phrase, the rise of the "black bourgeoisie."[20] This Negro middle class achieved prominence and wealth by serving the expanding Negro community. They were professionals, journalists, undertakers, real estate operators, and merchants. Their skills in medicine, law, and political life offered direction and leadership to the Negro community; they became the spokesmen for their people; in time, they produced eligible members for the upper-class élite of the Negro community, which cultivated the family traditions, educational standards, and style of life for the leaders of Negro society. The Negro community in the metropolis developed a social class structure which paralleled the stratification within the White community. These parallel social class systems were seldom crossed except by Negroes who were light enough to pass or by Whites who married into the Negro community; nevertheless, middle- and upper-class Negroes mirrored the values and tastes of the dominant White culture. It was within this new middle class that ambivalence toward the Negro community was expressed in a new religious style.

The Negro middle class rejects the second-class citizenship foisted upon it by the White community; consequently, it rejects its own identification with the Negro community. On the other hand, its success and future depend upon serving a Negro clientele, for it is financially dependent upon the Negro community. Middle- and upper-class Negroes identify with the majority White culture in education and style of life, but they lack access to that culture; for example, they cannot purchase homes in residential areas commensurate with their ability to pay, and, although they live in the best areas of the Negro ghetto, these areas are deteriorating before they have access to them. Their children are forced to attend schools in disorganized areas; in fact, they are subjected to slum conditions even though their parents are prosperous enough to afford the best kind of housing. The prosperous Negro has climbed the economic ladder, yet finds himself on the lower rungs of the social ladder; his economic future is bound up with the Negro community, yet his heart is fixed on achieving his birthright as a full participant in the opportunities of the White culture. The successful Negro knows that perpetuation of the Negro ghetto only postpones the day when full citizenship is really his; but at present there seems to be no escape from this separate Negro identity.

The ambivalence of the Negro middle class is manifest in their churches, which underwent marked changes with the emergence of the bourgeoisie. An organizational style appeared, the emotionality of the folk religion was rejected, services became formal and dignified; congregational life was elaborated in various activities and recreational groups; moreover, the committees, children's groups, men's and women's activities, and recreational interests of the organization church appeared full blown within the churches of the Negro middle class.[21]

The organizational style in Negro churches reflects the ambivalence of the Negro bourgeoisie in a special way. The organizational style emerged in the ethnic churches as a reaction to the dissolution of the ethnic community; the organization church among third-generation ethnics was, thus, a substitute for a fully ethnic community of identity. The organization church developed among the Negro bourgeoisie when the Negro community was still *the* community of identity; however, the Negro middle class and the Negro community were bound together by White discrimination and the dependency of the "black bourgeoisie" upon a Negro clientele. The Negro bourgeoisie rejected this identification with the Negro community, even though it had no choice but to continue an external association with it. The organization church provided a middle-class style of religious participation which insulated the Negro bourgeoisie against the rest of the Negro community without explicitly signifying a rejection of the hand that fed them. The organization church is, in this sense, not only a substitute for a natural or racial community of identity but also a buffer against the lower-class Negro community.[22] The organizational style is a middle-class style of association which excludes those who have not accustomed themselves to a middle-class style of life; consequently, churches of the Negro middle class could work toward the advancement of the race, yet deny their identification with the deprived Negro society by participating in a Negro church with an organizational style.[23] Formality of worship, organizational style, and white-collar motifs are much more entrenched in the churches of the "black bourgeoisie" than in the White middle class.

The embodiment of Negro ambivalence in the organization church is further confirmed by the religious identification of the upper classes in the Negro community; upper-class Negroes took the further step of becoming members of churches which were affiliated with the major White denominations; until very recently these were all-Negro congregations, but their ministry, rituals, and traditions were those of established, old-line denominations.[24] Thus, upper-class Negroes express full identification with the ethos of the successful White community without rejecting the Negro community, for organizational style is a buffer against the lower-class Negro religion, and identification with the major White denominations is a buffer against the Negro community; nevertheless, a member of a Negro church is still part of the Negro community. So long as these affiliations are made with largely Negro congregations, the new community of religious identity can be fostered without cutting all ties with the Negro people. The development of integrated churches should create a middle ground for movement away from Negro identity; the desegregated church is an additional step toward White culture and yet it represents a step toward racial equality and advancement of the Negro cause. Negroes can participate in desegregated churches of an organizational style as an act on behalf of the Negro community and, at the same time, advance toward the full citizenship of their birthright.

We still must account for the continuation of the Negro community despite the emergence of the organization church; in accord with ethnic experience, the organizational style should appear with the dissolution of Negro identity. It is evident that Negro identity had really collapsed when the organizational style emerged, but the Negro bourgeoisie were externally bound to the Negro community and seemed to perpetuate a Negro identity; actually, many middle-class Negroes rejected religious participation entirely because of its exclusive Negro identity and devoted themselves instead to the material values of the American ethos.[25] The organization church of the Negro middle class was actually a disguised rejection of Negro identity; however, it was not a sufficiently explicit rejection for many of the bourgeoisie. The real pool for middle-class religious activity among Negroes will probably come from the bureaucratic middle class who are finding white-collar jobs in governmental organizations and business offices; this new Negro middle class is much more like the constituency of the major White denominations than the deeply ambivalent Negro bourgeoisie. The organization church among both groups, however, substitutes a collective form of middle-class identity for a congregation which gave religious expression to the total life of an organic community of Negro identity. The organization church appears in the Negro community as the new style of congregation for those who are alienated from that community. Its very introversion insulates it against that community.

SECTARIAN RELIGIOUSNESS

The sectarian movement is different from both the Negro and ethnic experiences. The sect, like the Negro and ethnic church, rejects the organizational style but for different reasons. The sect in the metropolis is detached from any particular community; it is composed of rootless people. There are racial and ethnic sects, but there are also sects among White newcomers and older residents. The common element in sectarian groups within the metropolis is alienation from the dominant ethos of middle-class life. The sect creates a separate community of social identity by explicitly rejecting the ladder of economic success of the middle classes for religious identity. H. Richard Niebuhr, Liston Pope, Anton Boisen, and many others have noted that the sect is the church of the disinherited, the religious community of the alienated members of the lower social classes.[26]

The life of the inner city is a mixture of many things; nevertheless, its dominant note is poverty. But it is poverty with a difference, since it exists in the midst of plenty. With luxury all around them, people of the inner city rub shoulders daily with the inheritors of the American way of life, read, hear, and see the propaganda of plenty, yet live in rat-infested tenements. The affluent society holds out promise of a better life, but the inner-city masses catch only the aroma of plenty, missing its substance. Dope addiction, syndicated crime, pimps, and prostitutes clutter the streets of the slum neighborhood; juvenile delinquency is rampant; the sanitation department ignores the garbage-strewn alleys; the landlord makes a few grudging repairs, ignoring the leaky pipes and filth-encrusted walls. The inner city is a scene of deprivation and apathy; it is also the milieu of the sect.

There is little continuity, order, hope, or direction for families caught in the deprivations of inner-city life; consequently, they lack a meaningful principle of social identity. The economic ladder beckons with promise, but the promise is belied by facts, for most of these families lack the cultural, educational, and personal equipment to climb the ladder of achievement. Their former way of life has been disrupted by moving to the metropolis; there is no clear way ahead, no path to a decent, orderly life.[27]

The sect promises order in the midst of chaos; it assures the outsider that he is really an insider—an insider because of his religious identity, though with respect to the ladder of success and the powers in the community he remains an outsider. The sect rejects the American criterion of social identity as secular, worldly, and a creation of the devil. True life consists in loyalty to the Message and the community which the Message creates. The attractions of the overdeveloped society are transient pleasures which lead to destruction; the insiders will be outsiders in the Last Judgment; they have their reward now, but the poor shall inherit the earth.[28]

The sectarian identity has definite moral content as well as promise; it creates a new community and fashions a morality for the dispossessed. The strict morality of the sect distinguishes it from the more emotional holiness cults.[29] The cult is a momentary escape from the hopelessness of inner-city life; it releases feelings of frustration without organizing life in a constructive direction. The sect, however, is a grooved path to a new life; members of sectarian groups are held to a straight and narrow path despite the temptations which beset them. The disorder of inner-city life calls for clear-cut moral directives; life is too disorderly to be lived by nice discriminations; good and evil, right and wrong must be clearly distinguished; in fact, the relaxation of discipline at any point can mean the crumbling of the whole structure. A sect, like an Alcoholics Anonymous group, must keep a tight rein in the field of moral discipline.

Another characteristic of the sect is the certainty with which it handles the problem of good and evil. Contemporary Protestantism has struggled to redefine its certainties in relation to historical criticism of the Bible; however, such nice distinctions increase anxiety for those who live with the uncertainties of inner-city life; new translations of the Bible threaten rather than help; the uncertainty of marginal existence cannot be overcome with relative truths. The sect meets uncertainty with final, unchanging claims for the literal truth of the Message; it holds out sacred fact in the midst of uncertainty. The literalist bent in sectarian thought overcomes ambiguity through a clear and authoritative word; others may tinker with Biblical translations and fancy speculations, but the simplest believer can know the truth if he clings to the written Word.[30]

The sectarian religious identity thus creates a community of insiders from alienated outsiders; it discriminates sharply between the holy and the unholy.[31] The sect explicitly rejects the economic hope which dominates the American ethos; it creates a new community with a destiny in the "world to come" or in the "new world" which has already invaded the old. Brotherly love within the new community replaces the petty thievery and moral degradation which pervade the inner city; men and women gain self-esteem despite their poverty; in turn they are motivated to pursue a decent life in an environment which seems hostile to decency; moreover, their children are encouraged to a good life by threats of eternal punishment and promises of a just reward. The economic and scientific gods of the American way are rejected by the sect. Sectarian identity, in other words, is a radical protest against the middle-class identity of the dominant ethos of American life; it is truly a substitute for American identity. The sectarian cherishes everything which the dominant ethos rejects: the sect esteems otherworldly values in a society which lives for innerworldly satisfactions; the sectarian rejects the worldliness by which society judges him a failure and adopts an otherworldliness by which he triumphs; he replaces the American veneration of science, the white collar, and the slick magazine with simple truths and homely virtues.

Sectarian identity contrasts sharply with the identity of the ethnic community.[32] The ethnic community is a mode of transition to the ladder of achievement, a platform from which to mount the ladder. The sect is not a bridge to the ladder of success, although it may indirectly become such a bridge by disciplining the lives of the disinherited and preparing them for middle-class work. The sect explicitly rejects the ladder; in fact, it is a substitute community of social identity for those who feel outcast and untouchable because of their poverty. Poverty is not inherently demoralizing; by American standards, the majority of the world's population live in abject poverty. Poverty in the midst of widespread affluence, however, is demoralizing; it becomes a mark of failure and degradation; it designates the outcast.[33] The appeal of the sect in such a situation is precisely its rejection of the significance of success—its substitution of "spiritual" for "material" success, its apotheosis of poverty from the example of Christ. The sect, consequently, offers an alternative community of identity for the dispossessed in American society; it creates a bridge *out* of the world rather than a bridge *to* the American way of life.[34]

Sectarian identity also contrasts with the identity of the Negro community. The difference is well illustrated by the growth of sects among the lower ranks of the Negro community. Negro identity is forged out of the discrimination that obtains in relation to the White community. Negroes share the values, aspirations, and standards of the American way of life. They seek an identity within the Negro community only because the White community has defined them as second-class citizens; actually, the Negro community protects its people against the slights and injuries which they and their children suffer at the hands of the White community; thus, the Negro identity is an enforced alternative to membership within the White community. Sectarian identity, on the other hand, is created by deprivation rather than discrimination. Since deprivations are experienced by both Negroes and Whites, sects spring up among the lower social ranks in both communities; in each case, however, the metropolitan sect is a protest against the prevailing ethos and establishes a substitute community of social identity. The sect is explicitly an alternative to the American way of life, although its exclusiveness creates a superficial resemblance to the Negro church.[35]

The sect cannot adopt the organizational style. If it does, it renounces the basic principle of its formation, for recreational activities and business transactions reflect the interests of those who scramble up the ladder of success. The sectarian style fastens on the narrowly religious interests of its membership, concentrating its whole attention on prayer, worship, preaching, and moral discipline. Recreation signifies moral degradation in the inner city; such activity has no place in the holy community. The sect is a stabilizing community for its membership so long as otherworldly values are kept in the forefront; every tendency to frivolous activity undermines this principle of religious identity, jeopardizing the continuity of the sectarian community. The sect lacks a communal base in racial or ethnic communal life; it cannot express the interests of a "natural" or organic community. The sect is a new community of identity, offering a message of hope for those in need. Its religious interests would be compromised by other interests; consequently, the sect avoids organizational elaboration. The sect is at the opposite pole from the organization church.

The development of an organizational style seals the fate of the sect, but the transition from sect to denomination sheds considerable light on the significance of the organization church. Many sects unwittingly become bridges to the ladder of success by inculcating a disciplined life.[36] Individual members of the sect may advance socially, or a whole sectarian group may rise on the social ladder. When this happens the sect assumes the character of a denomination; that is, the marks of the organization church begin to appear—formalized services, a trained ministry in white collars, and a bustle of committees and activities. It is difficult to define the precise point at which a sect becomes a denomination, but organizational elaboration is a sure sign of upward mobility of the membership. When the members of a sect have passed from the ranks of the disinherited to the ranks of the inheritors of worldly success, their religious style begins to reflect this new identity. No longer needing or desiring a religious identity which rejects the ladder of success, they need one to validate their place on it.[37]

Deep strains appear within a sectarian group during a transition to organizational style. The vanguard of the more successful find their new worldliness undermined by the Message of the sect; their financial success smacks of worldliness; their middle-class life requires more flexibility in moral standards; and education creates additional conflicts with sectarian claims to certainty. Those members of the sectarian congregation who still belong to the disinherited are sustained by their religious identity; consequently, they reject the transition to denominational form. Clinging to sectarian religious participation, they form a splinter group, while the upwardly mobile members carry much of the leadership and a majority of the constituency into the denominational pattern. The organizational style wins out in the emerging denomination, for the sect has moved from religious community to organizational collectivity. Middle-class identity has triumphed; the religious insiders have become social and economic insiders.

The moralism and communal solidarity of the sect, as we have noted, are grounded in a special relationship to God—a special relationship sustained by loyalty to the Message and obedience to the moral law. Such a sectarian community can preserve its unique identity only if it insulates itself against the pressures of the surrounding world; such insulation, however, is almost impossible in a metropolitan area. When economic success transforms the religious insider into a social and economic insider, it becomes difficult for the sectarian to oppose a world that acknowledges him as one of its own. He cannot be an insider in both worlds. The transition from sectarian community to organizational collectivity marks a change in the social identity of the sectarian; he has surrendered his special religious identity for a religiously sanctioned identity on the economic ladder. The organization church gives a collective, religious sanction to his new identity. The sectarian is now an insider by his own achievement rather than by divine choice, and his religious style confirms this fact by placing a premium on his skills in committee work and fund raising. The organization church is, thus, a substitute for "natural" and/or religious communities of identity; it is a collective expression of social identity on the ladder of achievement.

The introverted life of the sect contrasts with the introverted organization church of the middle class. The sect is open to all who profess its faith; its prejudices are strictly religious, dividing people into believers and unbelievers; its work is missionary, as witness the rapid spread of the sects in Chile and in the metropolitan areas of the United States; its zeal has a religious center and a social class garb.[38] The organization church is also introverted, but on precisely opposite grounds. The organization church has a social class center and a religious garb; it is religiously inclusive but socially exclusive; its introversion is based upon social class identity and is therefore not missionary. In short, it is a secularized sect, a world set apart, whose distinctiveness is created by middle-class life, not faith. To say this is not to disparage the personal faith of members of the organization church nor to romanticize the faith of the sectarian. If secularization of the church is the substitution of alien grounds for its continuity, the introversion of the organization church is an instance of radical secularization. By contrast, the sect at its best represents one aspect of religious life which is needed within the denominational churches—the quality of faith and interpersonal community. The organization churches will require radical institutional changes in order to allow room for these dimensions of religious experience while still avoiding the cultural irrelevance of the sectarian group.

THE PLATFORM FOR MISSION

The chart on page 126 summarizes the factors in the transformation of ethnic, Negro, and sectarian congregations into collective forms. The crucial factor in each instance is the transformation in the criteria by which members of the particular group esteem themselves; lower-class ethnics, Negroes, and sectarians evaluate their personal significance in terms of their participation in "natural" or "special" religious communities, and their religious congregations represent these communities. When second- or third-generation ethnics or successful Negroes and sectarians begin to evaluate themselves by the criteria of economic success, their ties with the lower-class communities are broken and they seek a new center of identity; in each case, moreover, the new center of identity must accomplish certain things: the successful ethnic wants an "American" community with enough ethnic character to salve his conscience for betraying his ethnic background; the middle-class Negro wants a religious style which insulates him against his Negro identity and yet acknowledges formally his bond with the people upon whom he depends financially and to some extent emotionally; the sectarian wants a religious style more suited to the life of a worldly insider than that of a religious insider. The chart shows that the organization church, as the collective religious form of the middle class, has served the needs of each group in a different way, providing all groups with a religious sanction for their position on the ladder of economic success, insulating them against their background, and mediating a sense of identity on the basis of middle-class social status. The transition from "natural" or "primitive" community to the collective form of the middle class is simultaneously a transition from congregations which express the life of ethnic, Negro, or sectarian religious concern to the organization church. The transition outlined by the chart is, thus, a movement from community to collectivity, or from the church as representative congregation to the church as an introverted collectivity.

Transition From Congregation to Collective Organization

Variants of the Representative Congregation	Collective Form of the Organization Church
Outsiders—The Communities of Lower-Class Social Identity	*Insiders*—The Communities on the Ladder of Economic Success

Disruption of "Natural," Organic, or Protest
Communities of Identity

————————————————————————————→

1. Ethnic Congregation   Internally Oriented
   ——————→ Organization Church

(Middle Class of 2nd and 3rd Generations)

2. Negro Congregation   Organization Church of
   ——————→ Exclusive Negro Community

(Negro Middle Class)

3. Sectarian Congregation   Denominational Form
   ——————→

(Disciplined Economic Success of Members)

The disruption of organic communities and the appearance of mass society have usually been linked with the proletarian situation; thus, men are alienated from the means of earning their livelihood and become the mass of dehumanized labor—a commodity on the market. The preceding analysis suggests that the new middle class has experienced a similar alienation in industrial society; hence, the organization church emerges as the religious expression of this alienation and/or as a religious attempt to overcome the alienation. The religious significance of the organization church is determined by its relation to the alienation of the middle classes. The fact that the organization church is a collective rather than a communal form —an organization of activists rather than an interpersonal community—suggests that the congregation yielded to the collective form with the rise of the mobile middle classes.

The collective form—the introverted organization church—will become a vehicle of mission and ministry in the metropolis only when it assumes a representative character. Representation, however, is more than a matter of intention or will, for it requires an operative base within which a religious community can function. We have seen how ethnic, Negro, and sectarian churches of the older styles represented their particular communities in significant ways. Such "natural" or organic communities are rapidly disappearing in the metropolis. They are being replaced by mass communities of social identity which are organized along social class, racial, and religious lines. The representative role of the churches will be recovered only as they begin to operate from inclusive bases that reach across some of these social class and racial cleavages. The organization church has the potential for such inclusive extension when its activities are directed to mission and its working base for ministry is determined by inclusive sectors of the metropolis. When the churches become exclusively identified with the social class pockets of the typical residential area, their organizational potential for mission is transmuted into an introverted and collective form; the church then becomes an end in itself and completes the spiritual impoverishment of the middle class.

The chart also reveals a basic cleavage in metropolitan society. The major denominations have been augmented for a half century by recruitment from ethnic and sectarian churches. When these churches adopt an organizational style, they sever their ties with the lower classes. The blue-collar and white-collar schism of the metropolis is thus crystallized in the schism between sectarian churches and the major denominations. This schism, as much a matter of style of life and culture as of economic interest,[39] now cuts through the Negro community and complicates the division between Negro and White communities. The reconciling task of the churches includes the healing of both internal and external schisms. These are conjoined tasks of reconciling ministry, for the unity of the Church is restored to her again and again in her mission and ministry. The institutional expressions of this unity are tokens of the deeper unity which informs the Church.

The scandal of the metropolitan churches is a reversal of the Gospel message. The churches now embody the brokenness of the metropolis rather than its promise of renewal, a fact most evident in the struggle of the churches to overcome internal forces of segregation, and in the failure of the denominations to mobilize a missionary force for their Negro and White fellow Protestants who are now flooding into central city areas. The denial of ministry to these groups, should it continue, will go down in history as one of the great catastrophes of American Protestantism. Within a score of years, Protestantism will be fatally weakened as a significant religious force in the United States.

The representative church, anchored in an inclusive community that overcomes some of the sharper cleavages in the metropolis, is the minimal working unit for overcoming the schisms within Protestantism. When the congregation participates in the brokenness of society, while imaging its promise of reconciliation and renewal, its institutional form will once again become a vehicle of mission and ministry.

The first assembly of the World Council of Churches at Amsterdam coined the term "The Responsible Society." It was stated that the responsible society is a society "where freedom is the freedom of men who acknowledge responsibility to justice and public order and where those who hold political authority or economic power are responsible for its exercise to God and to the people whose welfare is affected by it."

"Responsible society" is not an alternative social or political system, but a criterion by which we judge all existing social orders and at the same time a standard to guide us in the specific choices we have to make. Christians are called to live responsibly, to live in response to God's act of redemption in Christ, in any society, even within the most unfavorable social structures.[1]

The foregoing statement from the Evanston Assembly of the World Council of Churches discusses the responsible society as a sequel to consideration of the unity and mission of the Church. It affirms that "Christians are called to live responsibly, to live in response to God's act of redemption in Christ . . ." It also affirms that living responsibly is applicable to life "in any society." The discussion of the metropolitan church has raised some serious questions about the responsibility of the churches: congregations are disengaged from answerable relations within the metropolis; they are autonomous bodies which claim to be answerable to God, yet seem to be answerable only to their own survival as organizations. The churches can legitimately address human society about answerability to God and man when they are ready to face as well the question of their own responsibility.

Many aspects of responsibility are involved; for example, the Evanston statement links responsibility to being answerable to God, the people whose lives we affect, and to Christ. A husband, for instance, would consider his relation to his wife in the light of

God's love and commandments, in terms of the consequences of his faithfulness or unfaithfulness, and as a reflection or denial of the love which Christ has shown for him.[2] These are familiar aspects of responsibility to most Christians; they can be taken for granted here. The difficult problem in the responsibility of the churches emerges in the *context of responsibility* rather than the *intention*; many churches have good intentions, yet few seem aware of the effects of their existence upon the community. Context of responsibility means the setting in which one operates and through which one becomes accountable for one's acts. A man may intend to be a good husband, but his intentions cannot be tested unless he marries. The problems of marriage and a home will define the context in which he will prove himself a responsible husband or not.

In order for a church to become responsible, it has to answer for the consequences of its actions, whether these be successes or failures, problems that were not anticipated, or relationships and alliances neither foreseen nor desired. This seems obvious, yet it is precisely what has been missing in the churches of the major denominations; they have been answerable to everyone and no one, to every place and no place. Limitations of time and space not only place a ceiling upon man's ambition but also provide the occasion of his responsibility. These "natural" limitations create the theater as well as the vehicle for his responsibility.

In a rapidly changing metropolis, a congregation is an evanescent thing; the ruling board of a congregation may vote to change the location of a church, yet every member of that board may sever his tie with the congregation within a decade. We have already seen abundant testimony to the fact that the churches have had little or no tie to local or metropolitan areas of responsibility; in fact, they have answered to no one in any immediate context of accountability. They have not, for example, lived with and answered to the working classes, whom they deprived of a ministry and ejected from the churches; they have certainly failed to answer to the Negro children, whom they excluded from their facilities. Human beings become responsible only within a context of obligations; the same is true of institutions, religious and otherwise. The Evanston statement has much to say to the churches, but the first question it raises is that of context.

The disengagement of the churches from responsibility for the metropolitan community came about as a consequence of social change; the neighborhood and residential area became a private sphere of life in an industrial society, yet religious congregations continued to center their memberships in this private residential sphere. The net effect was to insulate the churches within a privatized sphere—thus disengaging them from public responsibility.

PRIVATIZATION OF THE RELIGIOUS SPHERE

Protestant religious life underwent a series of significant changes on the American scene, changes which culminated in the metropolitan church. The Protestant movement started with congregations and established churches in the colonies; however, these establishments were never adequate to the needs of colonial life. The separation of church and state in the federal structure of the United States set the stage for voluntary participation in a plurality of religious groups. Protestantism, which in Europe had allocated responsibility to political bodies in order to maintain the religious pattern of the society, now found itself without any established religious pattern, for state establishments were dissolved in the early nineteenth century. The development of denominations transformed American religious life into a diversity of sects and religious traditions. When metropolitan growth was just beginning, the United States had become a scene of religious pluralism. Despite the religious competitiveness and overchurching of smaller towns, this pattern of religious activity was workable before the metropolitan development, for the congregation represented to some degree the life of the surrounding community. The political, economic, social, and cultural affairs of the community intersected in some significant way with the life of the congregation, whether the congregation took cognizance of this fact or not. American religiousness was multichrome in these early years but it existed within a context of responsibility.

Industrialization and metropolitan development changed this religious pattern radically; in fact, the loss of Protestant responsibility, although prepared to a degree by the disappearance of any established pattern of public responsibility, was really effected by industrial development. Several aspects of this loss of a context of responsibility can be isolated in summary fashion, since the effects have already been covered in the preceding analysis.

The congregational and parochial forms were defined by residential community in the Old World and the New; these forms, developed in the village and town life of medieval and Reformation Europe, fitted an agricultural and mercantile society. Residential community in this period coincided with economic, political, and cultural spheres of life; the household pattern of the village formed the hub for all community relationships.[3] Religious life articulated with this communal network either through the local parish or the representative congregation of believers; the business of the world and the life of the congregation or parish took place in a common arena.

In the past century, residential community has been segregated geographically, socially, and culturally from the economic and political structures of our society. This segregation of spheres of life in industrial society is the most important fact about social organization in the metropolis.[4] To be sure, political parties derive support from residential voting areas, but collective interests outweigh local considerations far more often, now that residential areas have lost much of their character and stability. Residential space is still the primary basis of the local school system; however, the major forces of cultural creativity, such as literature, mass media, and movies, do not coincide in any way with local neighborhoods. Perhaps more important than any other change has been the transformation of residential space into a reward for achievements in the economic enterprise; a high salary enables one to choose a suitable neighborhood. Residence has become the symbol of social position. Family problems, nurture of the young, neighborhood interests, informal association, and general consumer activities fill the highly insulated sphere of residential life.

The role of men in the neighborhood is a striking example of the degree to which the area of residence has become a private sphere divorced from industrial and, to some extent, significant political decisions in a metropolis. Men, and increasingly the large corps of commercially employed women, find themselves living in two distinct worlds—the occupational world and the sphere of family or related interests. Neither of these spheres is truly public, to be sure, since personal association is a matter of private affiliations and economic activity is a private struggle for existence. Nevertheless, a man's job is usually related, directly or indirectly, to large organizations of industry and union which have considerable influence on the national life; by contrast, his neighborhood, life with the family, at church, or in a local association has little or no connection with his job or even with the interests and problems which fill his mind through the day. The only significant tie between working life and residential activity today is that finding a desirable residential location depends almost entirely upon how well a person does in his job and whether he can hold it. Any other connections are coincidental; in fact, most men habitually empty their minds of job problems by the time they reach home. The sphere of residential activities is a very private aspect of modern life; whether this is good or bad is not of immediate concern here, since our principal question is what happens to the mission of the church when it is circumscribed by a private context of familial and leisure-time interests.

Religious activity undoubtedly affects economic and political activity indirectly by stabilizing local group memberships and sustaining the values and emotional balance of persons; this is equally true of marriage and accounts for the increasing concern of large companies over the marriages of their younger men who are being groomed for top positions. Whether the churches should affect economic and political interests directly or through stabilizing the values of local enclaves is not our immediate concern, for we are attempting to understand the process by which the mission of the church became circumscribed by the private interests of middle-class enclaves. One crucial reason for this circumscription of the ministry was the identification of the forms of church, parish, and congregation, with familial and residential interests which have become more and more restricted to problems of personal inwardness and emotional balance during the past century. This process has led to a restriction of the context of religious life to the most private matters.

In this sense, "public worship," as common liturgy in which the richness of the Word and Sacrament intersect with the common life of a people, has disappeared. We simply do not enjoy the experience of public worship, for the intersection of concerns in the religious context does not reflect public matters. To this extent, the proclamation of the Church occurs in an impoverished context which transmutes the Gospel into a superficial reinforcement of the moralistic façade overlaying the American pursuit of private interests.

Religious faith and practice have become a private sphere of American life—a sphere preoccupied with the emotional balance of the membership, the nurture of children, and the preservation of a harmonious residential milieu. Protestantism identifies the Church with a "gathered congregation" of believers, meaning a collection of individuals and families drawn from a specific residential area. Since suburban residential space provides the most stable atmosphere for the support of private interests, Protestantism has flourished in the segregated, suburban islands of private life created by the middle class. Where leisure interests and preoccupation with family values are dominant, religious institutions flourish. Where these values are undermined by inner city life, the ministry of the churches evaporates.

It is essential to recognize the radical change in Protestantism which has come with the confining of religious interest to the private concerns of residential life. The attentiveness of the churches to this sphere is certainly legitimate, but exclusive identification of religion with the private sphere creates a special culture in congregational life; the inevitable consequence is social irresponsibility, which means that the churches have abandoned a context of public accountability in order to serve exclusively the emotional needs of selected groups—those who are co-opted by the membership.

The denominations have a big investment in the parochial and congregational patterns of religious activity. This investment is not particularly rational, but it must be faced seriously. Since World War II the churches have spent hundreds of millions of dollars on facilities in the suburbs of metropolitan areas.[5] The pastorate to the segregated sphere of family life has exhausted the personnel and financial resources of the churches; despite these investments, the metropolitan sprawl has come about so rapidly that the churches will be unable to church new areas according to their present pattern. Finances and personnel are inadequate to continue this pattern of ministry to the private sphere.[6] The organization of religious life around the typical congregation or parish in a residential area may prove to be a morass in which the denominations will become mired. Local enclaves are multiplying more rapidly than the churches can serve them, which means that a ministry to private interests not only forecloses public accountability but in the end becomes self-defeating. Clergy experience this multiplication of private interests in their attempts to carry on a pastoral ministry in the modern congregation; the needs for personal help and counseling now tax whole staffs of clergy beyond their limits. There is no longer a significant context for congregation or personal life within the narrow confines of the privatized, residential interests. In their personal ministries, clergy become substitutes for the community they should be shepherding.

The most convincing evidence of the private character of residential life is the attitude toward racial integration in residential areas. Churches and residential associations have almost without exception opposed racial integration, while governmental, military, educational, industrial, business, and medical organizations have made progress toward it—though somewhat tardily, grudgingly, and in limited ways. It is worth noting that the same groups who encourage or accept desegregated practices in public spheres—for example, the labor unions—oppose the admission of Negroes to churches and residential areas; the same people, in fact, often hold contradictory attitudes in public and private.[7] The existence of this dual morality is a distinguishing feature of the metropolis. Public morality governs facilities, courts, and economic activity; private morality rules the spheres of housing, family nurture, religion, the elementary school, and in many cases the high school. The churches obviously have a significant role to play in directing these private spheres to greater social responsibility. There is no context for such responsibility, however, and even if such areas become socially more responsible, the churches will be insulated within a private sphere of emotionality and child care so long as they identify religious interests with local residential areas.[8]

A ministry to individuals and families in the context of residential association is no longer a ministry to society; in mass society, individuals contribute to decisions for the good or ill of the society, but they make these contributions through the managerial hierarchies, labor unions, community organizations, political bodies, and bureaucratic units which organize their lives. A ministry to individuals in a segregated residential area must be viewed as a subsidiary unit of a more inclusive ministry which intersects with public as well as private concerns of the society; the alternative to creating such a context of public accountability will be the continued captivity of the churches behind the suburban wall of privacy.

The exodus of Protestantism from the metropolis was a natural consequence of the restriction of religious institutions to private interests. It is essential to understand this. If we do not, two basic errors will be made in appraising the situation: (1) we shall assume that we can become responsible by moral exhortation; (2) we shall do serious injustice to the good faith of our forebears who instituted congregational life—imagining that we are somehow more faithful. The reduction of social issues to a choice between "good guys" and "bad guys" is endemic to American thought and obscures the real issues. Leaders of Protestant congregations who labored to preserve public worship and Christian instruction defined faith as right disposition, devout individual attitudes, and conventional moral observation; in their view social, political, and economic structures would be altered only when men had achieved the proper dispositions. Churches were voluntary associations in which men and women gathered for the inculcation of the proper dispositions, which were faith in God and love for one's fellow man. The leaders of these voluntary associations exercised responsibility by protecting the property and financial interests of the religious group so that the preaching and teaching might continue. In their terms, if a neighborhood became undesirable, it would be irresponsible to stay there; if admission of Negroes threatened to disrupt the voluntary fellowship, then better that a few should suffer than all be destroyed.

The exodus was an inevitable consequence of this view of Christian faith and church ministry—a view which conceived the church as a private institution devoted to the ennoblement of private life and to the amelioration of the ills of the society through individuals. A philosophy of religious activity with some meaning in the pre-industrial world became sheer irresponsibility with the growth of the metropolis; the preservation of congregational interests became a violation of the true mission and task of the church in the metropolis. The churches must now become publicly accountable institutions with a vision of the metropolis and their mission to it, for the day of the local congregation as a vital representation of the universal church has passed. The exercise of responsibility by pastors and laymen can now be seen, in the light of the altered situation, as social and public irresponsibility, although they acted in their time with good intentions.

The basic malstructuring of religious institutions which led to the exodus from the central city now determines the policies of the churches; in fact, the denominations are pursuing the exact pattern of private exploitation just described; the churches are becoming less rather than more accountable. There is no question but that religious pluralism aggravates this problem, even as the separation of church and state removes the political accountability of religious institutions. The leaders of the exodus from the cities cannot be blamed for acting on their understanding of the nature of the Church, but we are in a position to profit by the errors of their conventional wisdom and the policies it sanctioned.

How can the churches reverse the tide? Can Christianity ever be more than a private sphere of leisure activity in a society which separates religion from politics and economics, and uses it merely as a sanction for national values? Certainly the pluralistic religious situation plays into the hands of privatization, since no religious body can speak clearly amidst the present confusion of religious croakings.

The situation in England suggests that the privatization of religion has little to do with separation of church and state or religious pluralism. E. R. Wickham's analysis of the unchurching of working people and the development of private religion in England, so well documented in his book *Church and People in an Industrial City,* confirms our analysis of the role of social change in the disappearance of public worship.[9] The established church in England has fared somewhat worse than voluntary denominations in the United States. In both countries, work and worship, public life and religious interest are more or less segregated, although England's coronations, royal weddings, and other national fetes provide religious symbols that are lacking in the United States. The wide publicity given in the United States to the President's church attendance seems to be an attempt to capture some of this religious sanction for the national life. The issue in England and the United States, as Canon Wickham has amply demonstrated for the English situation, is the actual irrelevance of Christianity to the dominant spheres of life.

The issue in the United States is twofold: (1) to fashion congregational units which cross the racial and social class barriers that now embody the economic ethos and undermine the religious community; (2) to create at the center of these inclusive congregations a middle ground where economic, political, and metropolitan concerns can be discussed and faced in the light of the Christian Message. When devout Christians no longer meet their neighbors of different class and race because the economic ethos excludes such meetings, it is time the Christian churches established their own ground for meeting. When devout Christians admit, as many of them do, that they see no connection between their Christian faith and what is going on in their lives—particularly their work—it is time that the churches took a serious view of the working life of their members. Unless they do, they cannot fulfill their missionary role: proclaiming that Christ has broken the walls that divide men, and confirming His Lordship over all of life by extending their ministry to all spheres of contemporary society.

It would be difficult to do more than speculate on the creation of a richer context of responsibility in the metropolis if it were not for experimental ministries to the central city areas. Clergymen and laymen have worked for years to fashion a ministry for the inner city; some have worked through established parishes or congregations; others have created new forms of ministry; still others have initiated special ministries in relation to established congregations. Unfortunately, relatively little is known about these experimental ministries, and too little theological reflection has been directed to the new ground they have broken; enough is known, however, to suggest the direction in which the churches will have to move to shape the ministry to the metropolis.[10]

Experimental ministries in depressed areas of the inner city provide clues to the residential mission of the Church, since they are maintained under the most difficult conditions. The residential mission of the Church will be successful only if it can cultivate and sustain a broad, rich, and total mission to the inner city. Such a mission must emerge as an integral part of the daily life of the churches—not as an extra or special missionary "endeavor." To be the Church is to be involved in mission. To be the Church in the metropolis is to be rooted in the missionary task to inner city and suburb as an interdependent process. For our purposes, therefore, the Church in the metropolis requires forms in which inner city ministry is integral, not because the inner city is the most important part of the metropolis but because it is the test of an inclusive church. The inner city is a valuable testing ground, moreover, since the blight and demolition of this type of area spreads in ever-widening circles each decade.

We are forced to rethink the organization of denominational churches when we attempt to maintain a ministry in inner city areas. More than money and buildings are involved. Clergy in the inner city must feel they are a part of the total life of the Church; laymen must recognize that ministry in central city areas is part of their service to the Church. In other words, Christian ministry and life are more than putting a few dollars in an envelope. Such ministries are more than a gesture of good will on the part of a few members of an insulated enclave. In fact, the rethinking of total ministry requires a review of the whole pattern of ministry in the suburbs.[11]

To think in this way about the ministry to the metropolis reverses the usual process, for the churches now raise funds and make plans primarily according to the needs of the local congregations— for the most part, local needs in the better residential areas. After these expenditures, money is allocated to special ministries in distressed areas. We shall now attempt to reverse this approach by asking: what are the needs in the areas of most serious deprivation? When these are known, the problem will be to determine the form of Protestant organization that can best meet these needs without neglecting the needs of local areas. The immediate problem is not how practical this approach would be in the development of a metropolitan program. The problem is to determine the form of Protestant organization that makes most sense in the metropolis when one takes full account of the job that Protestantism has to do. There is strong warrant in Scriptures for beginning with the areas of greatest personal, physical, and social need—the poor of the earth—as the decisive point for estimating the form appropriate to the task. God's deed for men conformed to the human plight; the Church must also conform to that deed, and its mission achieve the form of the Servant.

THE INNER CITY AND THE INCLUSIVE COMMUNITY

The first thing the experimental ministries make clear is the fact that Protestantism has to be *present* in the inner city. Obvious as this seems, it is the decisive step. The experimental ministries *are* present. To be the Church is to *participate* in the world to which the Church is sent.

Each of the experimental ministries has moved toward *presence* in the inner city. A diversity of people live in the inner city, some of whom are church members. Many of the congregations in these areas, however, have insulated their members from the social conflicts of their environment. Where ministries have worked through these existing institutions, their first task has been to orient the congregation toward the community. Kilmer Myers expresses this task in the following way:

In undertaking this apostolate, however, the parish must have at least the following characteristics: (1) a clergy and lay staff willing to embark upon strange and often dangerous paths; (2) a concerned core of militant Christians which agrees with the parish priests that this apostolate is part of the Church's mission to the community.[12]

Within their different religious traditions, each of these ministries affirms this basic need for *presence within the community*. J. Archie Hargreaves says of the Church in the inner city, "It must be so thoroughly immersed in the situation that the people of the inner city cannot deem it an outsider. This means real identification."[13] Speaking of their ministry to the Southern mountaineer in Cincinnati, Michael Hamilton says:

I myself learnt the doctrine of the Incarnation: That in order to minister to people you have to come down or up to where they are, not to get shocked or surprised at what they are or do, but to start with them from where they are, and not where you might like them to be. God did not shout down advice to us humans over the ramparts of Heaven, but rather came down and shared our problems.[14]

The staff of Judson Memorial Church say of their ministry in Greenwich Village, "The chief thing was to be *present*, to be *available*, and to know how to speak a sensitive, relevant word, when the occasion permitted it."[15]

The inner city is a highly diversified area with many attractive and well-educated people as well as criminals and dope addicts. Existing religious congregations generally include the more stable segments of the population; moreover, every instinct militates against their sharing the lot of the unstable groups. Tenement living and danger to children make it doubly difficult for religious leaders to share the life of such neighborhoods. They too would much prefer to escape the effects of social disorganization, however much they may enjoy the company of the more stable groups in the area. The emphasis on *presence* and orientation *to* the community in experimental ministries arises from awareness that the churches cannot mediate a true identity to the congregation by insulating them against the community. To be the Church is to be present in the lives and struggles of a total community; any other mode of existence for the churches, however understandable in terms of the terrible cost of involvement, means that a social consensus of nice people has been substituted for the presence of the Church. The testimony of the experimental ministries is that life under the claim of the apostolic consensus means presence within the social conflicts of urban neighborhoods. This is the reconciling presence of the churches.

Ministries to the inner city are difficult and costly in every sense. Long-standing members of congregations are often hurt by the priority of this claim of the surrounding community over their own investments in the congregational life. Clergy and laity become involved in difficult and even dangerous situations; furthermore, concern with a neighborhood means involvement in social, political, and economic interests which conflict with the pietistic strain in American Protestantism. The leaders in these ventures would be the first to minimize the sacrifices involved in being *present* in the inner city. Nevertheless, it is a fact that sacrifices which cannot possibly be anticipated are implicit in such situations. This is true, however, of every human encounter. The response to another person is the recognition that his very presence lays claims upon one's own existence. The task of being present in the inner city, therefore, dramatizes and intensifies the dangers implicit in every human encounter.

By their presence in the inner city, the experimental ministries provide an ultimately religious ground of social identity. A remark by George Todd of The East Harlem Parish will help to illustrate this characteristic of experimental work.

One church stopped calling on youth in a new low-income public housing project after some of the young people came to a youth group meeting in response to visits from the church staff. In a scuffle, a church chandelier was damaged and a wall was marred. "We can't have youth who don't know how to behave without breaking up our nice group," one of the leaders said. This church with its upholstered furniture, grand pianos, and stained glass windows might yet discover that God would bless it in its true vocation if it were to make the youth of its parish welcome there, even though it might mean names scratched on its spotless walls and broken panes in the stained glass. Youth who never saw love in action have to test it for a long time before they believe it.[16]

One can readily appreciate the feelings of the congregation over this incident. No one condones the destruction of property, especially when his own sense of identity is involved in the preservation of such symbols. Nevertheless, this incident is not uncommon in a ministry to the inner city; in fact, a tragic sequence of such incidents is recorded by Harrison Salisbury in his study of delinquency.[17] The significant point, however, is that a sense of belonging in the human community is mediated to the delinquent gang through the kind of acceptance which George Todd advocates. Robert Spike's account of coping with a gang at Judson Memorial Church illustrates this process.[18] The staff is repeatedly tested by such groups who need to find reassurance of their acceptance. Kilmer Myers' account of dealing with gangs also illustrates how easily faith can be shaken when the leaders seem to be retracting their promise to stand with the group.[19]

The mediation of true social identity in the inner city is particularly difficult, for the dominant ethos defines the inner city resident as a failure. He has not succeeded on the ladder of achievement and must survive as best he can in a socially heterogeneous environment. Subcultures of racial and delinquent complexion offer alternative modes of identity, but each in its own way is narrow and destructive. Apathetic resignation characterizes many of those who sense their defeat under this dominant ethos. The churches meanwhile struggle through experimental ministries to mediate a sense of worth, dignity, and common humanity. Within the churches, many members would like to cling to the ethos of achievement and find in their religious membership a sense that they have not been defeated. This is the dynamic of retreat into an insulated religious association. Against these forces from within and without, the experimental ministries are affirming human worth and dignity; they are attempting to mediate by their presence some sense of belonging in Christ's community, and thereby in the inclusive community of mankind. Where trust, confidence, and acceptance are present in this ministry of pastors and laymen, a renewal of human community may come; racial and social differences may become sources of mutual enrichment rather than destruction. It is only within such an embracing consensus of belonging that the differences within urban life can become creative rather than destructive.

The question that emerges from this review of some aspects of ministry in the inner city is how Protestant religious ministry can participate in the ministry to the inner city; in other words, how do insulated suburban congregations participate in a ministry to inner city gangs, different racial groups, and different social class levels? How does the Church manifest itself as an interdependent community of the metropolis ministering to many different groups out of a common center without violating the legitimate needs for particular, unique, flexible ministries to local groups? Can the inner city ministry be integral to Protestantism or will it continue to be the experimental witness of a few heroic individuals? Note: the inner city will soon embrace the central city, so that one third to one half of the metropolitan population may be left with occasional, experimental ministries.

The obvious problems of inner city ministries, and, before long, of ministries to the central city areas, are finance and personnel. How can ministries be sustained in blighted areas without outside help or ministers who earn a living in other ways? Furthermore, how do you get competent men into those ministries and give them the moral support to stay there? One obvious way is to stake out an area of Christian responsibility from the outer edge of the city to the heart of the inner city along a major line of access or freeway.

This area, then, becomes the sphere of responsibility for a ministry—from blight to suburb, Negro to White, blue collar to white collar, down-and-out to privilege. Finances, buildings, lay and ordained ministries, time, and other matters would be allocated over this whole area by decisions of councils of representatives from the area. Such an area—call it an area of access or of organic interdependence—would constitute the basic unit of ministry and the minimal unit of the Church. It would extend its ministry outside the residential sphere but its minimal space would embrace a whole sector of metropolitan life along a major freeway. The specific way of bounding such a unit would, of course, vary with the character of the metropolis. The key to this conception is that the minimal unit of ministry will be a *sector* (or *cross-section*) of the metropolis. The Inner City Parish of Cleveland approximates this outline of a sector ministry.

The advantage of such a conception of the Church in the contemporary metropolis is that it places responsibility for the needs of an inclusive sector of the whole metropolis squarely within the life of the churches. Whether to sell or keep a building, shift a ministry, purchase a gym, set up a storefront are all questions that will be decided on the basis of the needs for ministry in the whole area of responsibility. Whether to enlarge or reduce staff in a suburb will be decided in terms of total needs and available personnel; moreover, these needs will be defined by inner city and central city problems as well as suburban interests.

How can such a unit of accountability be created out of the autonomous enclaves of Protestant religious life? Churches are organic unities; they do not fit the rational patterns of human contrivance. There are various ways to build units. One of the obvious, though less desirable, ways is along denominational lines. It is less desirable only because it involves partitioning of local communities, and yet it may be the most lively possibility. Although 50 per cent or more of all laymen seem to have lost interest in denominational loyalties, most religious leaders still think in these terms.

Particular denominations can create sector ministries by establishing central responsibility in cross-sectional areas. The interdependence of ministries over a sector can be established through representative fellowships from local congregations which determine the allocation of funds, distribution of lay and clerical ministries, and provision of facilities for a whole area; the fellowships of individuals and households would contribute to the support of this single unit which could be called a congregation of Christ's flock, a parish, or a diocese, depending upon the particular religious tradition. This inclusive congregation would determine all policy, needs, and ministries through a council of representatives; in some traditions it would be guided by a bishop; in others, by a leading pastor or presbyter. The crucial point is that local residential neighborhoods are too insulated in their concerns to provide an operating base for a responsible congregation; nevertheless, local groupings need particular ministries and nurture in the Christian life, and their particular interests deserve attention and respect. Each area is a focus for renewal of community, but that renewal cannot be seriously furthered without opportunities for interdependence over the whole area of which this community is a part. The collective unit or sector ministry would further rather than impede depth and community in local neighborhoods, for responsibility to provide a ministry in a sector would make local units accountable for their existence.

Several obvious problems confront any movement from the organization church to such a community of organic interdependence of ministries. Even if we overlook the pressing problem of pride and local autonomy and simply consider the enormous organizational problems of such an organism, the difficulties seem overwhelming. Each organization is, at present, seeking to expand its own numbers and facilities at the expense of the local community. How can such organizations be persuaded to consider organic interdependence as an expression of the true image of the Church for the metropolis? The whole idea sounds ridiculous in the light of the Protestant heritage of voluntaristic individualism and the parochial autonomy of our most catholic branches of Christendom.

Organic interdependence is the direction in which transformation will come; such interdependence can be developed by democratic processes through voluntary combinations of congregations, or through co-ordinated planning from the top. These are problems of organization and planning which we now know how to solve. Such interdependence has begun to operate in a few experimental ministries; it is bound to come and is the only way in which the heroic ministry to inner city areas can become more than an isolated venture of hardy souls. Such interdependence may develop initially through co-ordination of particular congregations among churches of the free church tradition. In the more catholic tradition it could come through diocesan reformation and the recovery of the true pastorate of the bishop. At present, bishops in the more catholic tradition are really metropolitans; they no longer have time or opportunity to exercise a true pastorate and a sacramental ministry. Their sacramental acts, with the possible exception of ordination, are largely mechanical and formal. The loss of significance from the bishop's office is only one of the many ways in which confinement of the churches to a private sphere has undermined religious culture. The recovery of the bishop's office and establishment of the office of metropolitan could well emerge in this process; in fact, the recovery of the presbytery in the Episcopal Diocese of San Francisco may be a step in this direction.

The most promising path to responsible ministry with public concern may well be the consolidation of ministries by supplementary ordinations; in this way churches of various denominations could construct a unit of ministry of organic interdependence.[20] The central issue is ministry, and responsible ministry is crippled by denominationalism. To be sure, problems of faith and order must be considered, since the Church is the language of God's testimony in the world, the sign of His love for mankind, and the earnest of His promise of the reconciliation of all men. The missionary task is the Church's very reason for existence. Nevertheless, the Church is not just another institution; in fact, her life is constantly subject to the will of Him who summons and sends her; thus, her ministry is always subject to evaluation in the light of her mandate. Our consideration of a sector ministry arises only from this kind of evaluation—the mission of the Church as seen in the light of the Message which forms her life and the faith which moves her. Supplementary ordination, new forms and special areas of responsibility can only be determined in this tension between the true Message and the mandate to be a reconciling body in the world; exclusive concern either with Message or Mission can undermine the accountability to God or the world by which the existence of the Church is determined.

Several obvious problems can be noted in connection with instituting interdependent ministries to sectors of the metropolis. Such a transformation is impossible so long as the churches conceive a local unit in terms of a church building, a large educational plant, and an autonomous budget. Most of the educational units are used for trivial activities except on Sundays, when they house religious education programs. This is not to say that the study and nurture groups are trivial, but only that such groups could meet in homes and smaller facilities.[21] The duplication of church buildings, moreover, simply concentrates the resources of the churches in brick and mortar. Strategically located cathedral-type churches could equally well serve the worship needs of whole areas of communities with modern means of transportation and access. The churches are operating as though the bus, car, and train did not exist; moreover, the "edifice complex" in the suburbs expresses interest in status rather than worship. A suburb or local community could operate with a chaplaincy from an office and employ an educational unit. This unit could have a chapel for special services, but the principal worship for the fellowship of households would take place in the central church from which the local chaplaincy emanated. Several large churches could provide centers of worship for a whole sector of the metropolis; moreover, local buildings could then be designed to meet the particular needs of different areas.

We are a long way from such transformation of Protestant religious life; in fact, we are now desperately expending funds for suburban buildings and staffs, having stripped the inner and central city areas of ministries and facilities in order to pour these resources into the suburban enclaves. Worship is now a private affair much like speedboating and fishing. The sector ministry or a similar development of an accountable context, with occasional "Church Weeks" during which the whole sector could discuss their problems, might be a first step toward the recovery of public accountability and public worship.[22] The ministry to the metropolis clearly points us toward a renewal of the form of the Church; such renewal can only be a response to the promise of reconciliation, an embodiment of the Message as Mission.

The rapid pace of metropolitan changes makes it advisable to consider radical changes in the pattern of religious organization; the fact is that few central city churches will survive the next twenty-five years without radical changes in membership and location. Renewal and redevelopment will undoubtedly change the residential pattern of most central city areas in this period. The problem of ministry to growing satellite areas will confront the churches with innumerable financial and organizational problems. The Bureau of Research and Survey of the Church Federation of Greater Chicago has been working for years under Richard Myers' leadership in order to devise a broad plan for ministry to suburban and central city areas; yet the planning for both of these sectors of the metropolis has still to be created. The difficulty of such co-ordination lies principally in the lack of inclusive structures which embrace both central city and suburban concerns. The rapid change in the populations of these sectors and the rebuilding of whole communities will make the next twenty-five years a strategic period for a radical reform in the mission to these areas.

The problem in developing councils to represent local congregations and parishes can be solved by developing a comprehensive community to meet future urban changes. These councils may initially be advisory, but in time they will have to co-ordinate expenditures and ministries. The situation is similar to the development of the European Common Market. Once strategic planning for a common market had been established, expansion of industry, changes in farming methods, new policies of foreign trade, and stabilization of currencies could all occur in the context of the new federation. Other nations of Western Europe were forced to move in a similar direction in order to maintain their interests. The free trade communities created the environment of an entirely different world. Sector ministries can have the same effect on new residential and political developments in the metropolis. Once a denomination or group of denominations has set the pattern for such a sector ministry, a new religious environment will be created. Each newly developed area will be assigned to the lay apostolate of a particular sector; in time, ministries to hospitals as well as political, economic, and communal spheres will follow. The rapidity of metropolitan growth makes the sector type of ministry in an inclusive community both necessary and possible.

We have already seen examples of central city churches which have built chapels on the outskirts of the city in order to accommodate members who were leaving an area of changing population. Soon after the chapel is well established, the central city church is sold and the congregation becomes identified with the chapel. This familiar pattern represents a strategic withdrawal in contrast to the panic and flight which many churches have experienced. The purpose of a sector ministry is to stop withdrawal and flight. Different types of buildings can be purchased, sold, or constructed in various parts of the inclusive sector to provide for local needs, but the all-important issue will be adequacy of ministry rather than congregational survival. Innumerable opportunities occur week by week in metropolitan areas for the creation of sector ministries. The alternative will be, in all likelihood, a continuation of the flight, an increasing loss in church properties, and a continuation of ministry on the basis of power to pay.

The ease with which new patterns of ministry can be constructed in the midst of rapid changes should not be taken as proof that a sector ministry will be an easy road to ecclesiastical success. Some religious groups may build successful churches while other groups talk about an interdependent ministry. The flight from the central city is continuing. The churches can recruit from this panic by setting up chapels behind the suburban curtain. We have seen from the exodus, however, that the net effect of this pattern has been costly and self-defeating. In the final analysis, experiments with the sector ministry, like the European Common Market, will undoubtedly have to be tentative steps toward co-operation and planning. However, once these steps have been taken, the possibilities for responsibility in the metropolis will pave the way toward an inclusive community, which is absolutely essential for breaking down the barriers that now divide people in the metropolis.

MINISTRIES TO NONRESIDENTIAL STRUCTURES

The inclusive social identity mediated through a sector ministry would undoubtedly alter the complexion of urban life radically; it is just such an embracing structure that R. C. Angell has suggested in urban organization, although he is not thinking specifically of religious structures.[23]

The rapidity of metropolitan change has created a mosaic of local enclaves, all of them attempting to salvage some private stability from the flux of contemporary events. The churches pursued their traditional identification with residential community while these enclaves were emerging; consequently, the churches find themselves in captivity to the private interests of middle-class enclaves. Many of these private interests are legitimate and deserve the attention of the churches; whatever new forms may emerge in Protestantism, some of these needs, such as Christian education for children and pastoral care, will continue to exercise the ministries of the churches.

Two principal questions have pressed our analysis to a consideration of new forms of ministry which can break out of this "suburban captivity": (1) the churches are ministering in a narrow context of accountability to the evanescent needs of an enclave—they lack a context of public accountability in the metropolis; (2) a ministry to the expanding inner city area requires a more comprehensive base than that provided by the local congregation or parish—the Church needs a platform from which to exercise full ministry to all sectors of the metropolis. In addition to these practical pressures for a platform of communal interdependence across social class lines, there is the disturbing problem of superficiality in congregational life. The appearance of the local enclave and the trivial character of much religious activity are interrelated; a Christian today may be searching for the meaning of his life but the local enclave simply requires him to fulfill some religious duties and associate with the same people he meets in other local associations. Until men and women are drawn into the missionary enterprise of the Church, they do not discover the meaning of their baptism; in fact, they gain little from Christian nurture groups beyond the feeling that something is wrong with their religious life, and they end up surrendering any hope of finding the answer to the question that brought them to the church in the first place. The sector ministry, or any other interdependent form of Christian community, is essential as a context of ministry and Christian experience; everyone who joins the Christian Church should have an opportunity to serve in the lay ministry, where he can answer for the faith that is in him and discover his true identity in Christ through sharing in His reconciling work. The breakthrough from a local enclave to a public platform of ministry and worship is essential for the renewal of the churches and for the recovery of the lay apostolate. The exclusion of laymen from serious ministry in the churches is an ironical development in the Protestant tradition, yet the captivity of the Church behind the suburban curtain transmutes the lay ministry into mere contributors to the machinery of the local organization.

A sector ministry is also an organization, for it is a co-ordination of ministries and contributions to the religious life of a cross-section of the metropolis; however, the content of the activity is changed, and laymen will find themselves working with juvenile gangs, meeting with a race-relations fellowship, or leading a group discussion of political problems and the Christian faith. The sector ministry, or any other truly inclusive form of the Church in our day, will extend the strengths of the organization church by using this pattern of co-ordinated ministries to provide a ministry to the whole metropolitan area. The real key to any such platform of mission will be the lay apostolate, yet paradoxically the Church can give birth to a true apostolate only as it moves out of its private enclaves into the public arena. In this respect, even the sector ministry is limiting to the Church as mission, for the sector too is a sphere of private, residential interests; in fact, there is no real center in modern life where the disparate interests of life intersect—the whole man and the whole community only intersect, if at all, in the inner life of the individual. The platform of mission must embrace other spheres of contemporary life if it is to provide a point of intersection for the whole of life under God.

Only through inclusive communities which transcend social class and racial lines can the churches exercise their reconciling ministry to the cities; nevertheless, congregations which reach from inner city to rural areas will depend upon a diversity of ministries to interlace their ministry with other structures of society. Ministries to industry, community, and political organizations should find their ground and support within the sector ministry. The sector ministries, however, must minister to nonresidential structures if they are to participate responsibly in the whole life of society.[24]

The diversity of spheres in contemporary life confronts the churches with opportunities and difficulties. The American tradition allows for pluralistic expression of religion, yet tends to exclude religion from economic, political, and educational spheres of life. This wall of separation is often unconscious, but it is assumed in most spheres of the society. The purpose of such ministries to special structures is not to impose a religious consensus on business or political life, but to manifest concern and to encourage responsibility in the fulfillment of the true tasks of these spheres. The environment, practices, and values of economic life now shape most facets of human existence; moreover, economic activity needs the Christian ministry of a self-conscious lay apostolate if it is to be a sphere of Christian responsibility. Ordained ministries to these spheres are only needed in order to mobilize and bring to awareness the lay apostolates. Spheres of life in which men spend most of their waking hours cannot be excluded from the scope of the ministry; in fact, the sector ministry may eventually find its ministry in the industrial sphere greatly expanded. Developments in this field are too new to visualize clearly the course that they will take. There is no question that ministries to universities and medical centers will develop on an increasingly wider basis; they should form an essential aspect of any platform of mission.

The enrichment of the form of the Church requires an intersection of special ministries with the interdependent ministries to sectors of the metropolis. The evangelical academies of Germany may well provide the patterns for this type of intersection, since they offer opportunities for laymen to consider all phases of life under God.[25] The Parishfield Community in Brighton, Michigan, has been engaged in lay training since 1949; however, most lay academies and training centers have existed without much involvement in parochial or congregational ministries, since there have been no inclusive structures with which to work. The emergence of academies without parish ties may have been necessary, since local congregations have been too insulated from other spheres of life to become engaged in such frontier work. It would seem, however, that in time something comparable to an evangelical academy will be needed at the center of each sector ministry. This calls for a staff of laymen and clergy to train and develop ministries for local neighborhoods and other spheres of life. There are innumerable possibilities for elaboration of such ministries, and the patterns may vary considerably with diverse polities and situations.

The task of the churches is mission to every area of human activity. The institutional forms of the Church are the modes of intersection between Word and world. Much as we might prefer the simpler coherence of the ancient institutions of village culture, that culture no longer exists. Our forms of ministry and patterns of engagement between Word and world must deal realistically with the society in which we live. The lay training center is not an additional nicety in a transformation of the churches; it has already demonstrated its power and significance in Europe. The sector ministry may even have to be initiated through just such a lay center; in fact, the academy may be the logical starting point of interdependence, since the academy or lay training center is by nature a center of dialogue. The crisis of the metropolis is essentially a crisis of communication; social class, racial, and religious groups are insulated from one another; most of the congregations of the major denominations have little or no idea of the suffering and despair of the inner city; few central city people realize the despair and depression which assail the suburbanite.[26] Breakdown of communication leads to deepening isolation and emptiness, creating a void in the political life of the metropolis. The academy, because it is dedicated to the practice of dialogue, is a platform of re-engagement. The development of sector ministries may well depend upon the unblocking of communication by the academies. In whatever form public accountability emerges, it will, however, express a message of reconciliation and an actual embodiment of reconciliation across the barriers of metropolitan life.

RECEIVING COMMUNITY AND MINISTERING FELLOWSHIP

The verdict on the organization church as a platform for mission is both "yes" and "no." Looking at the chaotic sprawl of the metropolis, we can only respect the remarkable staying power of the organization church. Reflecting upon the responsibility of the churches for the whole life of the metropolis, however, it becomes evident how narrow their interests are, how disengaged from the trouble spots of the cities. A mission to the metropolis can build on the new organizational form of the church only if it works from a more inclusive base and intersects with a wider scope of concerns.

Laymen in suburban churches are already trying to stake out a more inclusive base for their ministry. For example, a group of men and women in a Presbyterian church in Oak Park, Illinois, is already engaged in such a ministry. Laymen in the suburbs of other metropolitan areas are joining inner city churches in order to share the Church's mission within the metropolis. Many other clergy and laymen, of course, share indirectly in such ministries through special work on commissions and boards. These examples illustrate the concern of laymen for what is happening in the metropolis. These men and their families earn their livelihood in the cities, they know that the churches have responsibilities for the whole metropolis, and yet they feel excluded from opportunities to share in this responsibility. Even at the cost of leaving their suburban churches, laymen are responding to the need for an apostolate in the city.

The efforts of such lay groups need broadening through evangelical academies or lay centers in which other interests of the common life can be brought within the scope of their apostolate; in fact, the sphere of daily work is the central focus of the lay apostolate. Public accountability means participation by Christians as a believing community in the full scope of contemporary life. The ministry to residential areas is only one aspect of this involvement. Residential concerns and economic and political interests will have to intersect in Christian communities before the churches can adequately discharge their responsibilities. We do not yet know what kinds of Christian communities can best provide this ground of intersection.

The consuming and producing spheres of American society are now sharply segregated. The insulation of worship and religious community from the economic sphere of productivity is unquestionably the most important single fact about contemporary church life. A businessman noted this insulation in his own experience by pointing out that he had never detected any connection between his church life and business responsibilities in over twenty years of religious participation. He was undoubtedly a much better person as a consequence of his religious devotion, but he sensed that his business was alien territory. Consuming and producing communities can only intersect on common ground. The residential congregation of the consuming community must be far more inclusive to provide this point of intersection. We may not see such a point of intersection in our time, but the reconciling task of the Church in the metropolis will ultimately have to lead the churches to such a common ground.

The lay apostolate is foredoomed if its participation in the productive and political community is anchored in the segregated context of residential communities. We have seen ample evidence of this fact in lay movements based in residential enclaves, which invariably become large-scale facsimiles of the introverted activism of the organization church. With a few minor exceptions, this has been the fate of the lay movements which emerged in the American churches after World War II.

The renewal of residential life and the reconciling work of the churches in these consuming communities will require extensions of the operating area of ministry; this has been suggested by the sector ministry, but many other modes of extension are feasible. The congregation becomes a victim of the status panic unless the missionary task of reconciliation defines the area of its ministry. Even a full ministry in response to the religious search of middle-class people requires such an inclusive context for hearing the Gospel. The rectors of a White and a Negro parish in Detroit established co-operating programs in recent years simply in order to cross the racial gap. Many imaginative extensions like this will be needed before the broader outlines of an inclusive congregation emerge. Moreover, the racial cleavage is only one, and perhaps in the long run not the most difficult, gap to bridge in metropolitan life. The blue collar-white collar split may prove to be the Achilles' heel of the metropolis.

The renewal of life itself—the central task of the Church—demands of the churches a ministry to the whole of life. A productive society splits life; in fact, awareness of this split has penetrated to the deepest layers of the human consciousness. It emerges in the contemporary preoccupation with the dual world of "I-Thou" and "I-It," recently associated with the writings of Martin Buber. The personal world of I-Thou becomes a separate world. The renewal of life rests essentially upon the restoration of Thou-ness in all of life through God's work for man. At present, the churches attempt to proclaim the renewal of life in a segmentalized context that walls itself off from the producing community. The world of I-It becomes alien ground. Religious encounter in a bunker subverts the inclusive purport of the Message; the attempt of sacramentalists to enrich this context is basically sound, though the narrowed context impoverishes the liturgical life as well as the preaching.

The mission to industry, well established in Sheffield, England, and now developing in Detroit, Michigan, is an attempt to enrich the context of proclamation. The world of I-It easily becomes entrenched in the manipulations of the technical apparatus; a ministry scants the major focus of modern life when it looks away from this apparatus to the seemingly more personal activities of the residential community. In the long run, ministry in the apparatus will have to find a common ground with the ministry to residential life; the producing and consuming communities will have to intersect in the consciousness and concern of the Christian community. Until such an inclusive form of the Church emerges, the split in modern life will have sundered the religious community, imposed a cleavage in the Message which distorts its real meaning, and separated man even further from God.

The organization church, as a co-ordination of the ministries of members, has become introverted under the pressures which we have considered. Our conviction—and no amount of research could prove or disprove this—is that the majority of laymen in the organization church have been drawn there by a deep search for the meaning of life. Many of them could not put this search into words, and most of them would fail a theological examination. Nevertheless, underlying their search for social identity is a deep uneasiness which expresses itself in organizational activity. One indicator of the religious quality of this search has appeared in churches which practice racial desegregation. Despite the conflicts that have preceded integration, the average loss of members over this issue is infinitesimal. The organization church is introverted, activistic, often superficial, and too insulated from the public concerns of life, but, when the chips are down on personal and even some communal issues, a deeply religious quality begins to emerge. This quality needs cultivation, if the organization church is to break out of its vicious circle of introverted activities. Discussion of a sector ministry and a training academy is merely indicative of possibilities for such a breakthrough; even the hope of transforming the organization church into a missionary platform assumes that the members of the churches are searching for an opportunity to share in the life of the Church—a life which is essentially mission and ministry.

The organization church is an arrested form of development of the Church. Many forms of embodiment of the Church have emerged in the process of history—the New Testament household, the community of saints in Jerusalem, the medieval parish, the monastic communities, the mendicant orders, the Protestant congregation, the lay academies.[27] Each of these forms provided a mode of communion for Word and people and a vehicle of proclamation to the world. *A true form of the Church always appears as a mode of communion between God and man and a vehicle of mission to the world, for the ministering fellowship is simultaneously the receiving community.* The organization church is arrested at the stage of creating a viable mode of communion—a stable form for the receiving community in the changing metropolis. The introversion of the organization church is symptomatic of its struggle to survive as a receiving community; yet, this very introversion corrupts its nature and transforms it into a collective. The elaboration of this organizational form—staking out its area of responsible ministry across the lines which divide the metropolis—can renew the receiving community as a ministering fellowship. This is the crucial step in the evolution of the organization church as a true expression of the Church. When the receiving community becomes the giving community, its form will be true to the Church. For this reason, the organization church, despite its activity, is not really organized enough; it is an arrested form of the co-ordination of ministries in the missionary task.

The organization church can only evolve toward a true form of the Church if its formation is guided by the missionary task. Our common calling—the missionary task—presses us toward the proper form of our life, and is precisely the point in question today. Beyond their own survival, the churches evince little sense of their task in the metropolis; yet, this task alone can light the way to the true form of the Church in the metropolis.

SEVEN

The Renewal of the Metropolis

Citizens of the metropolis realize that their future and the lives of their children depend upon the creation of a safe, healthy environment in the metropolitan area. The exodus to suburbia has failed to check the spread of blight. There is no retreat from the disorder and deterioration which plague metropolitan society. Many of the new residential areas on the edge of the central city may be slums within a generation. Delinquency rates in the new residential areas are second only to those in the worst slums of the city.[1]

The metropolis is an interdependent community, even though it attempts to conduct its private life in independent enclaves. The impersonal interdependence of metropolitan life is ultimately founded upon the interdependence of people, and must find expression in communal and public responsibility. To deny this basic interdependence through discrimination, segregation, and social insulation violates the worth of people and ends in retaliation or mental withdrawal. The rejected child who becomes angry or withdrawn is the metropolis writ small, for he represents the denial of human worth, which transforms a citizen into a public enemy or public charge.[2] Somehow, and before too long, the metropolitan areas must face the task of rebuilding their local communities and integrating these communities in a public sphere; this means the creation of a community in the metropolis in which respect for all citizens is expressed through access to housing and interclass associations.

The churches bear a heavy burden of responsibility for the failure of the metropolis to become a community. Bishop Richard Emrich of the Episcopal Diocese of Michigan underlined the extent of this responsibility in discussing the racial question with a group of clergy a few years ago. He emphasized the responsibility of a church for the delinquencies of a Negro boy whom the church has excluded from its membership. The Negro's delinquencies may be caused by family and environment, but the White church in his neighborhood which refuses its ministry to him bears a considerable share of the responsibility for his crime. This interpretation of religious responsibility extends to all phases of metropolitan development—the ghettos, housing inequities, school deficiencies in slum areas, exploitation of newcomers by real estate and business interests, the disregard for life that permits residential areas to become highways, and the inadequate fire inspections in slum areas. The churches are not alone in this responsibility, of course, but they bear a large share of the burden. And the responsibility remains theirs whether they concentrate their ministry in the satellites or remain in the central city.

Urban planners, metropolitan councils, housing commissions, community organizations, and religious leaders have worked for years at the task of re-creating a sphere of public responsibility in the metropolis.[3] Religious leaders and pastors have felt the burden of this task with particular poignancy, for their form of religious organization is inadequate to maintain contact with the inner city and may well lead to their demise in the central city within the coming generation. Now, when the metropolis needs a publicly accountable and responsible leadership more than ever, religious institutions are withdrawing.

Our concern with religious institutions in the preceding analysis may seem to lay undue stress upon the role of the churches in the renewal of the metropolis. This preoccupation with religious institutions arises, however, because of their seeming helplessness before the forces of metropolitan blight. The churches are essential at this juncture in metropolitan development, for they can best represent the interests of the whole in the midst of conflicting economic interests, and can speak out most strongly for life and human values. The churches will fail to bring about a renewal of the metropolis, however, unless they first put their own house in order.

We have been concerned with the renewal of human life in the metropolis—the struggle of the immigrants and newcomers, the alienation of the Negro population, and the frantic search for tradition and security among the middle classes. Such concerns may seem nonreligious or irrelevant to the main stream of American Protestantism, which holds the object of religious concern to be individual piety and spirituality. This religious tradition assumes that preaching the Gospel leads directly to the reconciliation of society; the church's work, therefore, is to spread the Gospel and let social problems take care of themselves.[4] The only answer to this pietistic tradition is that the Gospel embraces the whole of human life and society. Man's life in society is an interdependent web. Personal immorality is no more nor less accessible to spiritual renewal than racial discrimination in housing. A narrow spirituality refuses to recognize the interdependence and wholeness of life; its concern rejects involvement, and its preoccupation with individual piety derives from the false assumption that the individual soul is more open to change than social institutions. The story of the Crucifixion demonstrates the cost of involvement in the torn web of human life, even as the Resurrection proves that involvement is the ultimate path to life. Individualistic pietism rejects the Cross. For a century the churches have disengaged themselves from the metropolis; that is, they have refused involvement with the plight of modern man. (The Negro boy can fend for himself.) But the Cross says *we are involved* here and now, whether we acknowledge it or not.

Our evaluation of metropolitan Protestantism scanted the beliefs and teaching of the churches. This neglect is partly offset, however, by the excessive emphasis on belief and ideology in most discussions of Protestantism.[5] American Protestantism views religious life almost exclusively as preaching, sacraments, and beliefs, and pays little attention to the social embodiment of this religiousness in the organizational forms of the churches; in fact, Protestant leaders scorn organizational structures, even though they spend most of their time maintaining outmoded organizational machinery.[6] This study, therefore, supplements a serious deficiency in most interpretations of Protestantism, since research on Protestant organization has hitherto confined itself largely to enumeration, and theological interpretations have slighted, if not ignored, the social organization of Protestantism.

Our concern with the social embodiment of Protestant religious life has been even more deliberate than our desire to supplement the superficiality of organizational studies and the neglect of social forms in Protestant theology. It is the firm conviction of the writer that the Protestant debacle in the metropolis—and it is hardly anything else—has come about through distortions in the social embodiment of Christianity. These distortions were caused in part by the organizational weakness of Protestantism, but even more by the pathology of industrial society. The doctor was not only infected by the patient, but also spread the infection.

THE DEFORMATION OF PROTESTANTISM

The main trends in the deformation of Protestantism have been set forth in this volume. These trends are symptoms of two kinds of estrangement in contemporary society: (1) lower-class sectarian, ethnic, and Negro churches disclose the alienation of the lower echelons of the working classes from the basic values of American life; (2) middle-class religious activity manifests the loss of identity by the middle classes through surrender to the demands of the American ladder of achievement. The lower classes are religiously disfranchised by the ladder of success; the middle classes are trapped on the ladder. American society is split through the middle by these two types of estrangement. The schism in Protestant religious life mirrors this cleavage as a kind of sickness within the religious body.

The task of the Church is reconciliation of men with God and with one another in human society. The ministry of reconciliation between blue collar and white collar, Negro and White, outsider and insider, central city and suburb is the work of the churches. Deformation of that ministry sets in when the churches crystallize and perpetuate the divisions within a society, lending sacred sanction to the estrangements which separate man from man. It is the churches' mandate to confess the dependence of men upon God and upon one another. When the sect proclaims an autonomous religious life and the organization church creates a middle-class enclave, the proclamation of dependence upon God is being used to deny dependence upon one another; the ministry of reconciliation then becomes a ministry of division and estrangement.

The desperate search for a community of identity among lower-class and middle-class people has twisted the churches into this ill-fitting shape. The churches, on their part, lacked the vitality and formative power to transmute this search. The sect and the organization church are both misshapen expressions of the search for identity, since the sect deflects the search into an emotional escape while the organization church dissipates the search in a vicious circle of activity. Industrial life drives the lower classes into apathy, making them a prey to psychosis and religious escape; competition on the economic ladder drives the middle classes into frenetic attempts to demonstrate their adequacy, which lead to despairing emptiness.[7] The apathy of the lower classes renders them inaccessible to the ministries of organization churches, for the manipulation of words and people in the organization churches is alien to lower-class life. This organizational style of religious life, on the other hand, is deadeningly familiar to the manipulated middle classes.[8] Thus, the cleavage within industrial society is mirrored in the styles of Protestant religious life.

Pastors experience the deformation of religious life most acutely in their sense of alienation from the significant spheres of contemporary life. Their ministries certainly touch the sufferings of private life—illness, death, familial estrangement—but they seldom intersect with the collective structures that shape the lives of their congregations.[9] At one time the parson stood at the point of intersection between the communal and private lives of his congregation, representing in his person the wholeness of God's concern for man and the fulfillment of man's life in God. Today, the pastor feels the deformation of religious life in being consigned to deal with a private sphere of symptoms rather than a public sphere of causes.

The pastor runs an ambulance service, so to speak—an important and indispensable aspect of the Church's ministry; but his services in this respect are performed without ever contacting the powers that shape the destiny of the metropolis and the world. Religion is now relegated to the sphere of personal emotional adjustment.[10] The metropolis perishes from the void in its public sphere; yet the pastors who sense this crisis are daily pressed more deeply into a private sphere of life, and end up tending the machinery of the organization and bandaging the bloodied heads. The crisis in the Christian ministry which is so often discussed stems largely from the dissipation of the ministerial vocation in private emotionality.

We have insisted throughout this analysis that the privatization of religious life—the deformation of the fullness of the Church into an attenuated religiosity—came about through the identification of congregational and parish life with residential and familial interests. A few centuries ago the residential parish embraced a public *and* a private sphere. The residential parish or congregation today is a strictly private sector. Pastors are trapped until more inclusive forms of ministry break through this wall of privacy. The churches suffer a damaging cultural lag; their adaptation of the village congregation to the metropolis has resulted in an organization church having a collective form with a private interest. The collective form alienates the lower classes, who want an urban form of the village church; yet the collective form is too exclusive to be a significant unit of ministry in the public sphere. The organization church is the collective expression of the private interests of a middle-class search for identity.

The deformation of the ministry is a religious symptom of the sickness of industrial society. Many successful pastorates exist under these circumstances, many faithful and devoted lives emerge from them; but the saints of the organization church are apt to appear despite the program rather than because of it. Notwithstanding the piety of individual pastors and laymen, Protestantism as a whole was vulnerable to the centrifugal forces of metropolitan life. The emphasis on voluntary congregations and individual piety made Protestantism a prey to these distorting forces. Each new stage of metropolitan disorder will manifest itself within religious institutions unless the churches assume a formative role in their ministry to the metropolis.

This analysis of Protestantism could be summarized as a loss of contact between the churches and the community as a whole. Their ministry, intended for the whole life of the metropolis, is increasingly fragmented to accommodate narrow enclaves. The choice confronting the churches today is whether to continue ministering to fragments of a society or to reform their ministry in order to participate in the whole life of the metropolis. It is a difficult choice, since the losses will be great in either direction; *ministry to parts* means continued frustration and the neglect of genuinely religious concerns; *participation in the whole* means organizing a new form of the Protestant ministry.

The conviction that reformation is the proper Christian choice has informed this analysis of Protestantism, but reformation would be unthinkable without the forces of renewal already present within Protestantism. In concentrating upon the social organization of Protestantism, we have necessarily slighted the powerful forces of renewal which are evident throughout Protestantism. Since Protestant religious life draws its power for ministry from the vitalities of congregational life rather than the fiat of hierarchical authority, it is essential to reformation that the forces of renewal be operative within the Protestant communities. The churches are experiencing a profound renewal of life out of the crisis of Western society which has infected their own social embodiment. In concluding our considerations of the role of the churches in the metropolis, it is essential to be cognizant of the power and direction of these forces of renewal.

RENEWAL IN PROTESTANTISM

The signs of renewal in Protestantism are striking. After almost a century of historical criticism, the modern use of the Bible is producing a vital theology. This new appropriation of the Bible already illuminates contemporary preaching and is revolutionizing Christian education. The insights of developmental psychology and group processes are being successfully applied to the teaching task of the Church. Pastoral care has benefited from the perspective of depth psychology, enabling the churches to respond magnificently to the infinite problems created by industrial development. Somewhat less extensive, though equally impressive, is the liturgical renewal that has begun to penetrate all Christian churches. Many branches of Protestantism, as might be expected, have been laggard in the reconsideration of symbols and sacraments; yet even in this sphere there are signs of new life and concern.

There are also signs of renewal in less conventional aspects of Protestant life, signs most immediately significant to the task of the churches in the metropolis. The most striking fact about contemporary Protestantism is the re-emergence of lay responsibility. Every attempt to organize this lay movement has resulted in shallow organizationalism, but the depth of lay concern is a continuing reality that will eventually provide the vitality for a new direction in the churches. In fact, if the lay movement were not already present in the churches, the groundwork of lay renewal would have to be laid now as the starting point for a renewal of the metropolitan church. The lay movement owes much to centers like Parishfield, Waycross, Kirkridge, and other newly developed retreat and camp fellowships. The lay apostolate has also been nurtured through parish-life conferences, study groups, and fellowships of prayer. Inchoate as it may be at present, the lay movement is a strong attempt to counteract the shallow activism of the organization church and to search for meaning and direction in a mass society. Many clergy have shied away from this lay movement for fear that it would disrupt the smooth pattern of church life, but those who have nurtured it have found new support for their ministries in sharing their task with laymen.

Two other signs of renewal can be noted in Protestant life. New ministries to the nonresidential structures of society are emerging: ministries to hospitals, universities, industries, and, more recently, to political organizations; furthermore, a ministry to the communal organizations of the cities has appeared in the form of church planning. The significance of these ministries, at present, is their concern with the structural problems of a mass society. Their potential power for renewal is considerable, since they signify the formation of a public ministry.

When the organizational weakness of Protestantism is seen in the context of so many signs of renewal, one is inclined to regard the social form as secondary to the vitalities already manifest in the churches. Why look at the bare bones—the skeletal structure of Protestantism within the metropolis—when the major denominations show unmistakable signs of vigor and new life? Unfortunately, the skeletal structure is essential to life, for it either preserves the vitalities or dissipates them. The organization of faith expresses or denies the Word to the world. When it expresses the Word, it channels the ministry into mission and servantship.[11] Renewal of mind is essential to the creation of a ministry to the whole metropolis; renewal of mind through the Spirit is the essence of life in the churches, and ministry is the vehicle of that life in the world. When the forces of renewal now present in the churches begin to shape the ministry, Protestantism will become the central force for renewal in metropolitan life.

THE FOCUS OF RENEWAL

The renewal of public responsibility and the creation of metropolitan community are two sides of the same coin. Each is essential to the other. When the churches suffered a breakdown of community as Christian people, the metropolitan area was deprived of the sustaining power of a faith that embraced the concerns of the whole. The collapse of the public sphere was almost inevitable without a community to represent the whole, for the free play of economic interests fragmented the metropolis, and no countervailing power represented the common good.

Perry Norton, urban planner and consultant of the National Council of Churches, notes this collapse of public life and underscores the Church's role as a guide to metropolitan community:

What are these issues and problems? . . .

(1) Slums are growing and they are increasingly the habitat of minority groups who are isolated and discriminated against, both in terms of housing and in terms of economic opportunities;

(2) Social tensions are reaching the explosive stages and we con-

tinue, doggedly, to ignore causes in favor of treating the results (e.g., juvenile delinquency);

(3) Social and political communication is almost at a standstill as the idea of responsibility is lost midst the welter of consumer-oriented propaganda;

(4) The concentration of urban populations is raising severe problems of water supply and the disposal of wastes;

(5) Open spaces are increasingly difficult to preserve, and the implications of this for food supply, standards (material) of living, economics of land development, and aesthetics are keeping many people awake nights.

. . . .

. . . There is a grim physical reality to the metropolis. From time to time we make pitiful token gestures toward its "problems." But no one guides us toward a *meaning* of community which comprehends more than profit taking and congeniality. Will the Church fill this emptiness in our society?[12]

To provide guidance toward metropolitan community the Church can: (1) affirm community by forming a ministry to the whole metropolis; (2) offer a vision and experience of metropolitan community by exemplifying a community; (3) inform the metropolitan struggle for community with its own prophetic concern for the common good of the metropolitan area. The deformation of Protestantism came about by the severing of its ministry from participation in the whole of metropolitan life; the reformation of Protestantism will come about through the participation of its ministry in the whole and the representation of the whole community in the communities of Protestant faith.

The renewal in Protestantism will be tested by the extent of its formative power—whether it can generate inclusive ministries to the whole metropolis. Many pastors and laymen are ready to participate in the whole life of the metropolitan area. Having tasted the emptiness of an insulated congregation, they are searching for opportunities to share responsibility with other pastors and congregations.[13]

The preceding chapter suggested a sector ministry as a way of forming a ministry to the whole—ministering to a representative cross-section of the metropolis. This was not offered as a blueprint, although it rested on the principle that ministry today means a struggle to participate responsibly in the whole community of the metropolis. The centrifugal forces of the metropolis shatter such ministries. It was also urged that intercongregational and interparochial councils be established for the allocation of ministries and funds, that the diversity of local ministries issue from a central community which grasps the needs of the whole and allocates according to needs, and that ministries move toward interdenominational unification by mutual ordinations. The central concern is ministry and mission; in metropolitan terms today, this means participation in the whole and breaking through the mosaic of insulated enclaves which shatter the public life of the metropolis. This is the only valid criterion for testing any reformation in Protestantism; its formative power will be tested by its assumption of responsibility for the whole.

Church planning, which has emerged in recent decades as a way of allocating new missions in efficient and co-operative ways, has been extremely useful as far as it has gone. Unfortunately, church planning has been preoccupied with extending the organization church in suburban and satellite areas. This pattern was challenged in the preceding chapter because it constitutes a denial of the axiom of mission in the metropolis—participation in the whole. The power of church planning is that it brings together agencies and groups who know the metropolitan picture and exercise responsibility for the action of the churches. Church planning, however, will fulfill its promise only when it regards participation in the whole metropolitan area as its essential principle, its first task the breakthrough of insulated enclaves within Protestant religious life. Sector ministry is only one among many possibilities for effecting a breakthrough, and commends itself largely because it embraces a manageable cross-section of the metropolis where blue collar and white collar, Negro and White, rich and poor can share a common ministry.

The metropolis is a mission field not because there are unchurched people but because there is no public ministry. By treating the metropolis as a Christian culture in need of supplementary church construction on the periphery, we are seeking to escape from the missionary task. Missionary strategy must concern itself with the whole. In no other way can it adequately express the Gospel of God's reconciling work for man. If a Christian culture informed the entire religious life of the metropolis, the support of that religious life would be the principal task of the churches. This analysis has offered incontrovertible evidence that the metropolis is a religiously broken, fragmented cluster of insular pockets estranged from one another. Its religious life is split through the middle by schism—a truly satanic division—and its religious organization upholds social class identities rather than the universal identity of those who are interdependent in Christ. We have, in fact, the strategy of an established church in a missionary situation.

The exclusive identity mediated by the churches today was illustrated by a suburban pastor, who announced from the pulpit that the suggestion had been made to invite Negroes into the community and he wondered how the congregation would feel about it. Although the question was put rhetorically, several members shouted No! No! When middle-class people cry out spontaneously in church in reply to a rhetorical question, one can be sure their deepest feelings have been touched. Their reaction was a full confession of their understanding of religious identity.

The Church proclaims a universal identity largely by involving its membership in experiences of obligation toward other people in the congregation. For many people today, church membership means the opportunity to see the same people they meet at Kiwanis or the country club. The Church will guide the metropolitan community toward the meaning of community when church members transcend the social, racial, and economic barriers that inhibit communication. These members may represent different local fellowships, since housing in the metropolis is more and more confined in particular neighborhoods to single social class levels, and no local fellowship can be all-inclusive. Their church membership, nevertheless, will be proof of their determination to disregard social barriers; it will mean the willingness to assume responsibility for financial and personal ministry in areas of radically different social and cultural background. A member of a suburban parish, for example, will perhaps spend one night a week in a slum mission or a household fellowship in exurbia. The Church communicates essentially by what it *is* rather than what it *says*. The Church speaks, as does Her Lord, from the reality of Her life rather than the imagination of Her heart.

The exclusiveness of identity communicated by the churches was illustrated a few years ago in Detroit, when a congregation met to discuss the evangelization of Negroes who had moved into the vicinity of the parish. The general opinion voiced by leading speakers at the meeting was that this congregation had worked hard to build and pay for *their* church; let the Negroes do the same for *their own* church.

A congregation that uses neighborhood boundaries to define a religious community is confusing social class and residential identity with the meaning of membership in the Christian community. Such parochial identity has spread the infection of communal exclusiveness in the metropolis. The true meaning of community will be expressed by churches and ministries only when they become representative cross-sections of the whole metropolis. No Christian unit can represent the Church in the metropolis—image the whole in any of its parts—unless it include blue collar and white collar, Negro and White. Such representative units of the whole may reflect many households and local fellowships, but the responsibility for ministry can no longer be vested in these isolated units, for they invariably become insulated under the centrifugal pressures of metropolitan life.

The task of the Church, then, is to participate in the whole by defining the metropolis as its mission field and unifying its ministries in inclusive sectors of the whole, and, at the same time, representing the whole in each of its basic units of responsibility. The test of the renewal of Protestantism and of its renewing power in the metropolis will be, thus, the formation in its own life of "inclusive communities," where the divisions of the metropolis are overcome. Protestantism now ministers to fragmented parts on the assumption that there is a metropolitan community; consequently, its ministry actually furthers the process of fragmentation. The churches will offer vision as they represent sections of a healed metropolis within their own communities, disclosing the reconciling power of the Spirit in the metropolitan struggle.

There are deeply divisive forces at work in the metropolis—forces which seem beyond the power of man to generate. Nevertheless, there have been occasions when the churches have successfully embodied a new order of fellowship amidst these divisions. The missionary and social impact of this new representation of community is beyond human calculation. For example, a Lutheran parish on the South Side of Chicago desegregated at the first sign of Negro movement into the neighborhood. Other churches around it were being sold. Attempts had been made to bomb a Negro residence. The whole atmosphere of the neighborhood changed, however, when this church made the step to integration. Today, some six or seven years later, that church is probably the only church on the South Side that is half Negro and half White, and exerts an influence in the community far exceeding its numbers. The metropolis looks desperately for signs of the true meaning of community, not simply in words or willingness to extend a missionary ministry, but, above all, in concrete terms of community and reconciliation.

It is evident from our analysis of metropolitan religious life that only the rare congregation can truly represent community in the contemporary metropolis, since most local congregations today are too exclusive. Everything militates against such community representation unless it is established on an inclusive and explicit basis of responsibility. Whatever form the representative community takes in the coming decades, Protestantism will participate effectively only as it represents the whole in its particular communities of responsibility. Local parishes and congregations used to be representative units—at least, in principle—of the communities they served, and were supported by the web of that communal life. Today, the deterioration of public worship and public responsibility has brought about a crisis of communication in the metropolis and simultaneously produced the organization church. The formative power of Protestantism will be tested by the courage it displays in breaking through the narrow confines of the organization church to a more inclusive form that images the true meaning of community for its own membership and the metropolis.

THE FULLNESS OF THE CHURCH

The problem of emptiness is the pressing issue of modern life. Even exurbanites confess that the emptiness which led to the exodus remains with them. In the final analysis, the overdeveloped society discovers emptiness and despair at the end of its struggle for productivity. Productivity without meaning is empty.

The churches, too, are experiencing emptiness. Struggling to preserve their position in the metropolis by frenetic building programs, their congregational life remains hollow. Recent attention to problems of unity has not filled the void, because these problems are tangential to those of contemporary religious life and divert attention from the problems of the Church in the world.[14] If true unity is to come in the Christian world, it will come through the fullness with which Christ's rule fills all of life—the fullness of the Church's presence in all parts of the metropolis and in all spheres of life. The recovery of public worship will be the first step. In a day of privatized religious concern, a kind of unity is possible for the churches by further withdrawing from the metropolitan struggle into homogeneous enclaves, but the true unity of an ecumenical Church—a universal community of faith and faithfulness—is possible only through the full realization of Christ's presence in all of life.

Our study emphasizes the need for reformation in the churches, so that they can begin to minister to all parts of the metropolis and all phases of contemporary life. Fragmented and broken, the metropolis pulverizes every communal form which strives to give coherence to its pattern of growth. Only a Church, therefore, which has committed its whole life and institutional forms to a flexible missionary strategy can hope to offset these destructive forces by the fullness of Christ's presence.

The general conclusion from this study of the churches is that the Church is deformed by the struggle to survive and reformed only as ministry and mission. It is an old and familiar notion in Christianity, but perhaps it has to be rediscovered by each generation of Christians as it contemplates its ministry and the form of its obedience. Difficult as it is to face the call to mission when one has settled like Jonah under a booth east of the city, the Church-as-Ministry, or the Church-as-Mission, is the only obedient and true form of the Church. The central principle of this book can be put in three words: reformation is mission. The true Church realizes its mission in the world by a continual reformation.

Mission and ministry witness Christ's presence in the world through the testimony of His people. Laymen who sense the emptiness of the organization church will discover fullness of faith only by sharing the ministry of a missionary Church, not the mission of co-optation which they have known. Fullness of faith means the risk of a church's life in ministry, for it is Christ's presence with those who minister in His name. Fullness of faith is evident in the experimental ministries to the inner city, which are helping people simply by their involvement and presence. Their obedience is a fulfillment of the Church's mission. It is also the essential life of the Church as witness to the fullness Christ brings to all things.[15]

This study of the churches in the metropolis documents the central principle of the Church's being: the Church as ministry. The tragic picture of city after city littered with decaying church buildings and multitudes betrayed by their own congregations underscores the fact that the churches die when they grasp at survival. The judgment on the churches is fulfilled as emptiness when mission becomes co-optation and ministry becomes sitting under a booth.

Historical judgments are necessarily partial judgments, both revealing and obscuring the ultimate. The Church lives by promise, bearing within itself the gift of mankind's redemption in Christ. In one sense, the failures of the churches are as nothing compared with the grace of Christ. In another sense, the churches fail when they obstruct the promise they are commissioned to proclaim and embody, for without a vision of community the metropolis becomes a scene of despairing conflict and empty defeat. The Church is justified neither by adequacy of faith, nor perfection of social organization, nor obedient testimony. The Church is justified, fulfilled, and sanctified to the world by the gift of the Spirit. What is given to the Church is hers only on behalf of the world. An image of hope, guiding mankind to the true meaning of community for the metropolis, the Church is no mere servant of man but a gift of the Holy Spirit.

If this study has stressed too exclusively the burden of witness, it is a fault; for the Church lives by faith and promise, even as the form of her life is mission and ministry. To recognize the nature of the Church as a divine gift is to find courage and hope for the task ahead—the renewal of the metropolis.

Acknowledgments

This analysis rests on collections of data from diverse sources, representing unequal degrees of validity and representativeness. The author is grateful for the opportunity to benefit by this research; yet he is also aware of how tentative many of his generalizations are because they could not be tested in the framework of a large-scale research program. Piecing together bits of evidence, even when done with extreme caution, as in this analysis, cannot take the place of representative research. Such samples do not exist at this time, however, and assembling them will be very costly.

After completing this manuscript, the author was privileged to read a series of new research reports which include data of very high quality. W. W. Schroeder completed an account of the Bureau County research in Illinois, which he submitted in partial fulfillment of the requirement for the degree of Doctor of Philosophy at the University of Chicago under the title, "Religion in a Midwestern County: An Empirical Investigation of Ecclesiastical, Theological, Sociological, and Psychological Factors." This research enriches our whole understanding of the religious life of the United States and adds considerably more detail than the present analysis. The general tenor of Schroeder's analysis suggests that the interpretation given here would apply with slight modifications to the town and country areas.

Yoshio Fukuyama has submitted a thesis as partial fulfillment of the requirement for Doctor of Philosophy at the University of Chicago under the title, "Major Dimensions in Religious Membership," which is an analysis of styles of member orientation in a sample of twelve Congregational churches. This research was completed soon enough to be noted in the body of this text, but the broader implications of the research will be most significant in the sociology of religion. Clearly confirming the dominance of the organizational style which had been discerned from the studies of

H. Paul Douglass, Fukuyama's thesis reveals the correlates and significance of this organizational style in their full import.

Finally, the author had the privilege of reading the first draft of Gerhard Lenski's monograph on the familial, economic, and political aspects of the religious life of the Detroit metropolitan area. This is one of the most representative studies of religious life available and will add significantly to our understanding of this field. Several broad findings of the study illuminate this analysis and can be indicated here. The word "Protestantism" is useful in distinguishing a tradition that contrasts with Jewish and Roman Catholic associations and subcommunities. The cleavage between Negro and White Protestantism is very sharp and is the major distinction to be made in the Protestant cluster. Blue-collar ranks are represented in Protestantism, but active Protestants tend to share very markedly the middle-class orientation to life. This has been known intuitively and even on the basis of ecological data used in the present analysis, but Dr. Lenski's work substantiates it strongly. His study also introduces one qualification into the preceding analysis. Religious traditions are indirectly creating definite patterns of value orientation which he traces with controlled indices. The private sphere of religious interests informs political and economic life indirectly through the value patterns which it supports. This is not a new notion, but the delineation of these patterns and the estimate of their diffusion is of the greatest importance. Broadly speaking, Protestantism sanctions the traditional ethos of free enterprise in American life—essentially the middle-class system of values—and supports the liberal tradition of civil liberties. It is only when one questions the economic ethic of this tradition, believing that it was creative in the nineteenth century but not now, that one begins to question this pattern of indirect support of middle-class values. It is mainly on this basis that the present author questions the privatization of religious life. Protestantism in the United States merely sanctions the American ethic of achievement.

The present study would have been greatly enriched by the aforementioned researches, for they clarify our understanding of the religious life of the United States. On the other hand, the privilege of examining these studies prior to publication of this analysis gives greater confidence to the present author, for many reconstructions and tentative generalizations will receive fuller statement, adequate qualification, and positive validation in these new materials.

The author is most directly indebted to the researches of the Institute of Social and Religious Research. This Institute was guided in urban research by H. Paul Douglass and in rural research by Edmund DeS. Brunner. We confined our attention to the work of Mr. Douglass, although Mr. Brunner's continuing influence was felt in all of this research. By 1934 the Institute had completed 48 research projects and had published 78 volumes. The works of the Institute cited in this analysis are designated by the italicized parenthetical dates in the following citations: *The St. Louis Church Survey*, by H. Paul Douglass (New York: G. H. Doran, 1924) (*1924*); *The Springfield Church Survey* (New York: G. H. Doran, 1926) (*Spring 1926*); *1000 City Churches* (New York: G. H. Doran, 1926) (*1926*); *The Church in the Changing City* (New York: G. H. Doran, 1927) (*1927*); *The Protestant Church as a Social Institution*, by H. Paul Douglass and Edmund DeS. Brunner (New York: Harper & Brothers, 1935) (*1935*); *The Metropolitan Pittsburgh Church Study, 1948 Report*, by H. Paul Douglass, *et al.*, in Swift Library, University of Chicago (*1948*); *Minneapolis Churches and Their Comity Problems*, by Wilbur C. Hallenbeck (Institute, 1929) (*1929*); *The Strategy of City Church Planning*, by Ross W. Sanderson (Institute, 1932) (*1932*). Most of these studies done under the auspices of the Institute are summarized in *1935*.

Notes

CHAPTER ONE

1. *The Exploding Metropolis* by the Editors of *Fortune* (Garden City, N.Y.: Doubleday, 1958).
2. *The Structure of the Metropolitan Community* by Don J. Bogue (Ann Arbor, Mich.: Horace H. Rackham School of Graduate Studies, 1949), pp. 6 ff.
3. For an account of the emergence of the city, see *The Rise of the City* by Arthur M. Schlesinger (New York: Macmillan, 1933); for figures on urbanization, see "Urbanism in the United States" by Don J. Bogue in *Cities and Society*, edited by P. K. Hatt and A. J. Reiss (Glencoe, Ill.: The Free Press, 1957), pp. 83 ff.
4. The Bureau of the Census in 1950 defined a Standard Metropolitan Area as a "county containing a central city of 50,000 or more inhabitants plus any adjacent counties that also appear to be metropolitan in character and socially and economically integrated with the central city." See Don J. Bogue, op. cit., p. 93, which considers "principal" metropolitan areas from 1900 to 1950 with populations of 100,000 or more.
5. *The Structure of the Metropolitan Community*, op. cit., p. 19.
6. *The Changing Shape of Metropolitan America: Deconcentration since 1920* by Amos Hawley (Glencoe, Ill.: The Free Press, 1956), p. 2.
7. "Residential Distribution and Occupational Stratification" by Otis D. Duncan and Beverly Duncan in *Cities and Society*, op. cit., pp. 283 ff., and esp. p. 295.
8. *The Negro Population in Chicago* by Otis D. Duncan and Beverly Duncan (Chicago: University of Chicago Press, 1957), esp. Table 1, p. 24.
9. "The Church and Segregation in Washington, D.C., and Chicago, Ill.," (by Frank David Dorey unpublished Ph.D. dissertation Chicago: University of Chicago, 1950). The spatial concentration of Negroes was unaltered during the in-migration of Negroes from

1920 to 1940 (see Chapter One). See *The Negro Population in Chicago*, op. cit., for detail.

10. *The Metropolitan Area as a Racial Problem* by Morton Grodzins (Pittsburgh: University of Pittsburgh Press, 1958).

11. Ibid., p. 12.

12. See *The Structure of the Metropolitan Community*, op. cit., for a brilliant analysis of this pattern of interdependence. Don Bogue concludes his summary of this process by quoting with approval the statement of N. S. B. Gras ("Interdependence of parts is really the key to the whole thing"), p. 63.

13. *The Social System* by Talcott Parsons (Glencoe, Ill.: The Free Press, 1951), Chapter II and *passim*, for an analysis of instrumental and expressive patterns in interaction; this analysis undergirds the notion of impersonality in the metropolitan pattern of interdependence.

14. *The Ghetto* by Louis Wirth (Chicago: University of Chicago Press, Phoenix Books, 1928 and 1956).

15. "Urbanism as a Way of Life" in *Community Life and Social Policy*, selected papers by Louis Wirth (Chicago: University of Chicago Press, 1956), p. 116.

16. *Why Families Move* by Peter H. Rossi (Glencoe, Ill.: The Free Press, 1955), pp. 38 f. The author stresses mobility of areas as crucial to variation in intra-area sociability. The finding on higher degrees of sociability in higher-status areas despite mobility needs much more careful study in following some of Rossi's clues, but the principal contrast is between heterogeneity and homogeneity when one moves from a low-status to a high-status area. Mobility increases *perceived* heterogeneity and limits association.

17. "Two Worlds of Church Life in the United States" by Glen W. Trimble, in *Information Service*, published by Bureau of Research and Survey, National Council of Churches, Vol. XXXVIII, No. 7, p. 1.

18. *Yearbook of American Churches for 1958*, edited by Benson Y. Landis (New York: National Council of Churches of Christ in the U.S.A., September 1957), p. 281.

19. *Church Comity* by H. Paul Douglass (New York: Doubleday, Doran and Co., 1929). See Chapters I–III for a study of the development of co-operative church extension.

20. Quoted in *Information Service*, op. cit., Vol. XXXVII, No. 15, p. 3.
21. Ibid., p. 4.
22. The New York *Times*, Mar. 15, 1959.
23. Ibid.

CHAPTER TWO

1. *Social Mobility in Industrial Society* by Seymour M. Lipset and Reinhard Bendix (Berkeley and Los Angeles: University of California Press, 1959), Chapters II and III.
2. *The American Class Structure* by Joseph A. Kahl (New York: Rinehart, Sec. Ptg. 1959), pp. 72 ff.
3. Simply stated, this is the zonal hypothesis set forth by E. W. Burgess in *The City* by R. E. Park, E. W. Burgess, and R. D. McKenzie (Chicago: University of Chicago Press, 1925), Chapter II; this hypothesis has been subject to much criticism but provides a useful descriptive statement.
4. *The Changing Shape of Metropolitan America, Deconcentration since 1920* by Amos H. Hawley (Glencoe, Ill.: The Free Press, 1956), pp. 161 f.
5. See 1924, op. cit., Chart 19, p. 71, for the movement of White Protestantism in St. Louis; for Springfield, Mass., see *Spring 1926*, op. cit., pp. 72 f.; and for the situation in Chicago in 1945 see *Comparative Study of Congregational and Other Protestant Churches in Chicago, 1945–1946* by A. T. Rasmussen (Chicago Congregational Union; mimeographed copy in Hammond Library, Chicago Theological School), pp. 53 ff. and 71 ff.
6. Redevelopment areas, for example, such as Hyde Park-Kenwood in Chicago, eliminate low-cost housing by demolition and rebuild with private capital to the top income level within the area. Such areas can continue to support churches of the major demoninations, but this type of redevelopment is slow and costly.
7. *The Rise of the City* by A. M. Schlesinger (New York: Macmillan, 1933), pp. 330 f. and esp. footnote 3 for references.
8. Joseph Kahl, op. cit., p. 259; note the decreasing importance of foreign immigration after 1920 and the increasing significance of Negro in-migration from rural areas.

9. H. Paul Douglass and Wilbur Hallenbeck documented this process in their studies; see references to the unchurching of lower-class Protestants in 1924, op. cit., pp. 46–71; *Spring 1926*, op. cit., pp. 41–45, 274, 296, 298; 1927, op. cit., p. 412; 1929, op. cit., Charts XVI–XVIII, pp. 33 f.; 1932, op. cit.; reference to Hallenbeck's findings that in a supposedly Negro area left by Protestant churches, one third to one half of the school pupils were native-born White; 1935, op. cit., pp. 250–53; Walter Kloetzli has drawn attention to this problem among the Lutheran churches in a study on congregational structure, where he notes that a central area of Chicago with 800,000 population which once had dozens of National Lutheran Council churches now has three and these are new missions. The working-class areas of the metropolis were literally denuded of churches of the major denominations with the exception of a few high-prestige outposts.

10. The most detailed and convincing evidence of this process of central city losses and suburban gains was presented in 1948, op. cit., Table XLIX, p. 156.

11. In a study of 1044 city churches, the median age was 42 years and the median age of occupancy was 25 years, 1926, op. cit., pp. 232 f.

12. 1924, op. cit., p. 224.

13. See A. M. Schlesinger, op. cit., pp. 330 f.; it would seem from W. Hallenbeck's study that Protestant churches left areas long before the balance of Roman Catholic population was such as to make the area untenable (see 1929, op. cit., pp. 69–72 and *Spring 1926*, p. 299). Thus, the definition of a Roman Catholic area (and, as we shall see, a Negro area) is psychological and not statistical.

14. *The Social Systems of American Ethnic Groups* by W. Lloyd Warner and Leo Strole (New Haven: Yale University Press, 1945), Chapter VII; *Protestant–Catholic–Jew* by Will Herberg (Garden City, N.Y.: Doubleday, 1955), Chapters II and III; *The Uprooted* by Oscar Handlin (New York: Grosset & Dunlap, 1951).

15. 1924, op. cit., pp. 68, 73, 217; 1926, op. cit., pp. 251 f.; *Spring 1926*, op. cit., p. 281; 1948, op. cit., pp. 156 f.

16. 1924, op. cit., p. 65.

17. H. Paul Douglass notes this fact in many of his studies, but the appendices of 1948, op. cit., detail the proliferation of small

churches in the lower socio-economic areas of Pittsburgh. It is notable that seventeen denominations account for 96 per cent of the Protestant church membership in Pittsburgh (p. 63); yet those denominations have shown relatively little growth since 1930 while the sects increased their membership disproportionately with little effect on the total Protestant membership (pp. 11 f., 87, 89, 189).

18. *Some Social and Economic Characteristics of the Detroit Area Populations, 1952* (Ann Arbor, Mich.: The Detroit Area Study, mimeographed, 1952). Table I, 5, p. 19, shows that migrants of less than 17 years residence are 73 per cent Protestant to 21 per cent Roman Catholic, and of those from the South, 93 per cent are Protestant (Table II, 5, p. 29).

19. "The Role of Socio-Economic Factors in American Fundamentalism" by Everett L. Perry (unpublished Ph.D. dissertation, University of Chicago, 1959).

20. "The Church and Segregation in Washington, D.C., and Chicago, Ill." by Frank David Dorey (unpublished Ph.D. dissertation, University of Chicago, 1950), pp. 62–115 and Chapter V.

21. *The Protestant Church and the Negro* by Frank S. Loescher (New York: Association Press, 1948), p. 66; *The Kingdom Beyond Caste* by Liston Pope (New York: Friendship Press, 1957), pp. 108 f.

22. "Community Turnover on the South Side of Chicago" by Frank David Dorey (unpublished B.D. thesis, Chicago Theological Seminary, 1942), pp. 65 f.

23. This process is most clearly disclosed in the Pittsburgh situation, 1948, op. cit., Table XLIV, p. 156 and Appendices, but the present construction is hypothetical and needs further testing.

24. This is hypothetical in terms of other experiences, but it is supported by 1932, op. cit., p. 165.

25. *The Negro's Church* by B. E. Mays and J. W. Nicholson (New York: Institute of Social and Religious Research, 1933) points out the lack of contact between Negro and White churches and ministers in this period; the same situation is suggested in 1948, op. cit., see *Recommendations*.

26. *Where Shall We Live?* Report of the Commission on Race and Housing (Berkeley: University of California Press, 1958), Chapter III.

27. *An American Dilemma* by Gunnar Myrdal (New York: Harper, 1944), Chapter 40; *The Negro in the United States*, by E. F. Frazier, Rev. Ed. (New York: Macmillan, 1957), Chapter XIV, pp. 354 ff.; *The Religion of Negro Protestants* by Ruby Funchess Johnston (New York: Philosophical Library, 1956), pp. 175 f.; and on ministerial training, *1935*, op. cit., Chart XII, p. 113.

28. Morton Grodzins, op. cit., Chapter I.

29. *The Strange Career of Jim Crow* by C. Vann Woodward (New York: Oxford University Press, 1955); "The Political Role of the Church as Defined by Its Parishioners," by B. R. Ringer and C. Y. Glock, mimeographed, confirms this trend to conservatism among the religiously committed, less educated (generally lower middle class), and poorly informed members of the Episcopal churches; this is precisely the group in denominational churches that flanked Negro movements.

30. Otis D. Duncan and Beverly Duncan in *Cities and Society*, op. cit., p. 295, notes this high rent-income ratio among lower white-collar households in Chicago.

31. *Where Shall We Live?* op. cit., pp. 19 f.

32. Tenure of city pastors has been relatively short, but the differences in length of stay fit the general financial level of the churches. See *1926*, op. cit., p. 218; *1935*, op. cit., p. 117.

33. Research on the churches amply documents these generalizations; *Spring 1926*, op. cit., pp. 72 f., 299; *1932*, op. cit., p. 12; *1935*, op. cit., pp. 251 f.; *1948*, op. cit., pp. 156 f.

34. *The Renewal of the Church* by Visser t'Hooft (London: SCM Press, 1956), pp. 69 ff.

35. *Church and People in an Industrial City* by E. R. Wickham (London: Lutterworth Press, 1957), esp. Chapters II–V.

36. *Religious Behavior* by Michael Argyle (Glencoe, Ill.: The Free Press, 1959) Table 9, p. 37; also E. R. Wickham, op. cit.

37. It should be evident that the theory of turnover of membership in the major denominations is constructed on the basis of changes in church sites and concentrations of unchurched people in central areas of the city. This construction now leaves the unresolved problem of Protestant growth to be considered.

38. *1924*, op. cit., pp. 176, 241; see also *1932*, op. cit., pp. 85 f.; H. Paul Douglass noted several times that this new membership was more nominal than participant. We undoubtedly have a transfor-

mation in the nature and meaning of church membership from 1870 to 1950 which inflates membership figures and conceals the central city losses.

39. *Work and Authority in Industry* by Reinhard Bendix (New York: John Wiley, 1956), Chapters 4 and 6; *The Changing American Parents* by Daniel R. Miller and Guy E. Swanson (New York: John Wiley, 1958), Chapter Two.

40. *White Collar* by C. Wright Mills (New York: Oxford University Press Galaxy Book, 1956), Part Two, esp. Chapter 4; "The Middle Class" by Lewis Corey in *Class, Status, and Power* (Glencoe, Ill.: The Free Press, 1953), pp. 371–80.

41. Joseph Kahl, op. cit., p. 202.

42. Lewis Corey, op. cit., pp. 372 f.

43. Joseph Kahl, op. cit., p. 100.

44. Figures for the percentage of the work force in middle-class occupations for 1870–1940 from Lewis Corey, op. cit., p. 372. For 1950, figures are estimated from Joseph Kahl, op. cit., p. 67 and middle income group already noted; this is an underestimate judging from the fact that by 1957 the number of white-collar workers had exceeded the manual workers in the U. S. (Seymour Lipset and Reinhard Bendix, op. cit., p. 85).

45. Joseph Kahl, op. cit., pp. 264 f.; Seymour Lipset and Reinhard Bendix, op. cit., p. 88.

46. Protestants outnumbered Roman Catholics on a 2:1 ratio from 1870 to 1900; this ratio decreased in subsequent years, as shown in figures drawn from *Year Book of American Churches, Edition for 1958*, edited by Benson Y. Landis (New York: National Council of Churches of Christ in the U.S.A., September 1957), pp. 286 ff. No brief is held for these figures, although they are the best available, since other studies are not representative. The assumption underlying the estimates in Table 1 is that Luther Fry was correct in his analysis of the figures for 1906–26, which claimed that adult church membership kept pace with population increase: *U. S. Looks at Its Churches*, (New York: Institute of Social and Religious Research, 1930), p. 3; see also "A Guide to the Literature on Statistics of Religious Affiliation with References to Related Social Studies" by Benson Y. Landis, *Journal of the American Statistical Association*, June 1959, Vol. 58, esp. Sec. 7. We are concerned with the recruitment of the major denominations from the

middle classes, but these percentages include all Protestants. Actually, the 26 largest denominations included 92 per cent of all church members in 1890: *Eleventh Census, 1890,* Vol. 9, p. XVII; the 19 largest denominations included 88.7 per cent of all church members in 1936: *Census of Religious Bodies, 1936,* Vol. I, Table 13, p. 86. Smaller sects and denominations are numerous, but they account for fractional parts of actual church membership.

47. C. Wright Mills, op. cit., p. 65.
48. *Information Service,* op. cit., Vol. XXXVIII, No. 7, p. 1.
49. Roman Catholics were also moving into the middle-class ranks, although not as rapidly as members of the major denominations because of ethnic limitations; for Roman Catholic figures, see *Religion in 20th-Century America* by H. W. Schneider (Cambridge, Mass.: Harvard University Press, 1952), Table I, p. 228.
50. Lewis Corey, op. cit., p. 373.
51. Local studies suggest that the old-line denominations have actually lost members relative to population growth. This was true of the major denominations, with few exceptions, in the study of Pittsburgh for 1930–46 (see 1948, op. cit., Table XVIII, p. 89); the more recently rural and somewhat lower-class and the more recently sectarian forms showed gains in Pittsburgh. This is very suggestive, since it indicates that Protestantism might have shown serious net losses from 1870 to 1950 if the ranks of the major denominations had not been replenished from the upward movements of sectarian groups to denominational status and the increment of ethnic and semirural Protestantism. In brief, the exodus has cost the major denominations enormous losses in membership which are partially concealed by the appearance of new denominations. It should be clear from this analysis that the phrase "major denominations" designates a broad, religious orientation with a constantly shifting constituency of denominational bodies, some fusing in mergers and others emerging from sectarian ranks (see Chapter V).

CHAPTER THREE

1. This is a familiar phenomenon to clergy, although it has not been adequately studied. The unconscious middle-class rejection of

lower-class people was clearly demonstrated in public clinics of New Haven, where psychiatrists unconsciously avoided lower-class patients; see *Social Class and Mental Illness* by A. B. Hollingshead and F. C. Redlich (New York: John Wiley, 1958), pp. 344 ff. The parallels between psychiatric practice and ministry have become very explicit in the development of pastoral theology. An instance of exclusion of lower-class people in middle-class churches is included in a study of a war-boom community; see *The Social History of a War-Boom Community* by Robert J. Havighurst and H. G. Morgan (New York: Longmans, Green, 1951) pp. 176 ff.

2. The marketing personality and the self-alienation of the new middle classes have been discussed by C. Wright Mills, op. cit., esp. Part Three, "Styles of Life"; see also *Man For Himself* by Erich Fromm (New York: Rinehart, 1947), esp. pp. 67 ff.; note also the importance of feelings and subjective states in the middle-class groups: A. B. Hollingshead and F. C. Redlich, op. cit., esp. p. 240. This activism is traced in the churches in Chapter Four; for activism and patterns in the lower middle class, see *Family and Class Dynamics in Mental Illness* by Jerome K. Myers and Bertram H. Roberts (New York: John Wiley, 1959), pp. 45 ff.

3. J. K. Myers and B. H. Roberts, op. cit., pp. 49 ff.; Joseph Kahl, op. cit., pp. 210 ff.

4. Gunnar Myrdal, op. cit., pp. 573 f. This principle is usually stated as equality of opportunity, but in an industrial society the key to the arch is economic achievement.

5. The limitations on this market are discussed in *The Great Transformation* by Karl Polanyi (Boston: Beacon Press, 1957), Part Two.

6. *Protestant–Catholic–Jew* by Will Herberg, op. cit. Chapter V, where the author makes an excellent case for the fact that the religion of Americans is the American way of life, which has been described here as the American creed.

7. *Man in the Modern Age* by Karl Jaspers, translated by Eden and Cedar Paul (Garden City, N.Y.: Doubleday Anchor Books, 1957), pp. 49 ff.

8. Academic aspects of the market are touched in *The Academic Marketplace* by Theodore Caplow and Reece J. McGee (New York: Basic Books, 1958) and *The Sociological Imagination* by C. Wright Mills (New York: Oxford University Press, 1959).

9. A detailed analysis of the economic integration of the churches of the major denominations will be given, but the basic pattern can be seen in *As You Sow* by Walter Goldschmidt (New York: Harcourt, Brace, 1947), Table 24, p. 136; *Democracy in Jonesville* by W. Lloyd Warner et al. (New York: Harper, 1949), Table 13, p. 154; *Protestant and Catholic* by Kenneth Underwood (Boston: The Beacon Press, 1957), Table XXIII, p. 400, and note the even more sharply stratified character of Roman Catholic congregations in Table XXIV, p. 400.

10. Earlier studies of urban Protestantism indicate this trend to middle-class ranking, but the suburban exodus accelerated the development of the pattern: note, for example, the middle-class character of the churches of the major denominations in 1924, op. cit., pp. 105, 122; 1932, op. cit., pp. 15, 227 f.; *Spring 1926*, op. cit., p. 302. In a recent study of Congregational churches, Yoshio Fukuyama found only 8 per cent below white-collar level.

11. 1926, op. cit., p. 257; *Spring 1926*, op cit., p. 257; 1932, op. cit., p. 14.

12. H. Paul Douglass notes an interesting example of this phenomenon in Springfield, Mass. See *Spring 1926*, op. cit., pp. 286 f., 301.

13. *Spring 1926*, op. cit., p. 302; 1932, op. cit., p. 229; the Pittsburgh study, 1948, op. cit.

14. A. T. Rasmussen found in a study of Chicago churches in areas of social blight that 13.7 per cent of the members lived within one-half mile and 19.6 per cent within one mile. Op. cit., p. 89.

15. 1924, op. cit., pp. 64–71; *Spring 1926*, op. cit., pp. 41–45, 274, 296, 298; 1927, op. cit., p. 412; 1935, op. cit., pp. 250–53; 1929, op. cit., pp. 69, 72.

16. Michael Argyle, op. cit., pp. 123 f., 150.

17. Frank D. Dorey (Ph.D. dissertation, op. cit., pp. 235–44) found that only 23 out of 137 churches of the major denominations in Washington, D.C. were in below-average areas, almost none in the poorest areas.

18. H. Paul Douglass formulated this phenomenon as "like environment, like church," but this way of looking at the churches could not explain the prosperity of Negro churches in poor areas. Mr. Douglass had actually detected the working of economic integration, which is a social-class, not an environmental, condition; see 1935, op. cit., 247 ff., 254.

19. This reason is often cited to explain Protestant difficulties in desegregating their congregations; see, for example, *Pious and Secular America* by Reinhold Niebuhr (New York: Charles Scribner's, 1958), pp. 82 f., where as acute an observer of the American scene as Niebuhr assumes that the "chummy fellowship" is the issue in Protestant desegregation. Note that desegregation occurs in Protestant and Roman Catholic churches where the Negro membership is of equal or higher status, whereas churches in transitional areas of invasion have uniformly resisted integration; see *The Protestant Church and the Negro* by Frank S. Loescher (New York: Association Press, 1948), esp. p. 79.

20. A *Theology of the Laity* by Hendrik Kraemer (Philadelphia: Westminster Press, 1958), pp. 131 ff.

21. "Co-optation: A Mechanism for Organizational Stability" by Philip Selznick in *Reader in Bureaucracy*, edited by Robert K. Merton et al. (Glencoe, Ill.: The Free Press, 1952), pp. 135–39.

22. *1948*, op. cit., p. 203 and Table LXV, p. 205.

23. Studies of such webs of interaction by W. Lloyd Warner, A. B. Hollingshead, and others have been summarized by Joseph Kahl, op. cit., Chapter V.

24. *Childhood and Society* by Erik H. Erikson (New York: Norton, 1950), esp. p. 228 for a definition of the sense of ego identity; see also *Mirrors and Masks* by Anselm Strauss (Glencoe, Ill.: The Free Press, 1959) for elaboration of relations of ego identity to social identity.

25. Will Herberg, op. cit., has set forth a convincing thesis on the role of the three major faiths in the search for social identity in the United States. The present analysis is indebted to Mr. Herberg but is primarily concerned with the form of the New Protestant religiousness as an expression of a middle-class identity.

26. The excessive participation in associational life by the middle classes is well attested in the literature. See J. K. Myers and B. H. Roberts, op. cit., pp. 48, 52; see also "Urban Structure and Social Participation" by Morris Axelrod in *American Sociological Review*, Vol. 21, No. 1, Feb. 1, 56, Table 3, p. 15. Studies by Gerhard Lenski and Yoshio Fukuyama indicate that organizational participation in the churches correlates highly with general associational participation.

27. In Erik Erikson's terms, the dominance of productivity and social approval as a means of establishing identity stresses "generativity" (op. cit., pp. 230–34). This emphasis in congregational life follows from the rule of economic processes in the society or the transformation of the society and public life into a process of collective housekeeping. See *The Human Condition* by Hannah Arendt (Garden City, N.Y.: Doubleday Anchor Books, 1959), Part II; the congregation, in this sense, is a microcosm of the society—an example of perpetual housekeeping.

28. The uncertainty and sense of dependence on an impersonal fate are very marked in the middle classes. The reaction of residents of Dearborn, Ill., to a plan for integrated housing reflected this anxiety: they said they simply could not risk this threat to their property, which was heavily mortgaged. A similar occurrence in condemning property purchased by a Negro in Rutledge, Pa., was reported in the Washington *Post and Times Herald*, Mar. 14, 1959, B-2.

29. There have been a few noteworthy instances of racial integration, such as Salem Lutheran Church in Chicago, but the over-all picture in the churches, despite the radical shift for integration after World War II, has been one of little or no change; see *Kingdom Beyond Caste* by Liston Pope (New York: Friendship Press, 1957), pp. 188 f.

30. Relatively little attention is given to the steady defeat of Protestantism in the central cities. Dr. Robert A. McKibben of the Methodist Church spoke frankly on the problem in Boston; see the New York *Times*, Sun., Mar. 15, 1959, p. 70. Bishop Angus Dun of the Episcopal Church in Washington, D.C., has also faced up to this question; see the Washington *Post and Times Herald*, May 5, 1958, where he is reported to observe that the Episcopal Church, which has done more toward integration than most other denominations, had only 100 Negro members in the 96 churches of the diocese.

31. *The Racial Problem in Christian Perspective* by Kyle Haselden (New York: Harper, 1954), where the "right to belong" and the true interdependence of Negro and White are incisively stated. A theological statement of this interdependence of true identity is to be found in *The Image of the City* by Charles Williams (Lon-

don: Oxford University Press, 1958), pp. 102 ff. Denial of interdependence is, in this sense, impoverishment of one's own being and identity. The impoverishment of the churches of the metropolis as a consequence of their denial of lower-class and Negro people has already been documented in Chapter Two.

32. Delinquency is intimately bound up with the disorder of inner city life and will not be controlled until community is re-created in central city areas; see *Towards an Understanding of Juvenile Delinquency* by Bernard Lander (New York: Columbia University Press, 1954) for a discussion of the role of Negro-White relations in the genesis of delinquency; see also *Free Society and Moral Crisis* by R. C. Angell (Ann Arbor: University of Michigan Press, 1958) for an interpretation of the seriousness of the inner city crisis; see also an analysis of the search for social identity in delinquency in "The Darwinian Model in Social Analysis" by Gibson Winter, to be published in the Chicago Divinity School volume on "Evolution," edited by Jerald Brauer.

CHAPTER FOUR

1. For a careful analysis of organization, see *The Organizational Revolution* by Kenneth E. Boulding (New York: Harper, 1953); note in Chapter 12 the discussion of power by Reinhold Niebuhr.

2. *The Living and the Dead,* by W. L. Warner (New Haven: Yale University Press, 1959) p. 234.

3. The studies of the Institute of Social and Religious Research, as noted in the Acknowledgments, provided the principal data for the study of activities. Although much more research is needed on this style of membership, Yoshio Fukuyama's data confirm the dominance of this style in the contemporary life of the denominations.

4. 1926, op. cit., is the most detailed study of this phenomenon.

5. 1935, op. cit., Table IX, p. 137, provides a contrast between the town church (pop. 2500 to 5000) and the modal city church (pop. over 5000).

6. 1926, op. cit., p. 271.

7. 1948, op. cit., pp. 158–61.

8. 1935, op. cit., p. 94.

9. "Rural Ministers" by S. W. Blizzard et al. in *Science For the Farmer*, Vol. V, No. 4, Spring 1956.

10. *The Purpose of the Church and Its Ministry* by H. Richard Niebuhr in collaboration with Daniel Day Williams and James M. Gustafson (New York: Harper, 1956), pp. 90 f.

11. 1926, op. cit., Chapter XI; 1948, op. cit., pp. 158 ff.

12. *Why Families Move* by Peter Rossi (Glencoe, Ill.: The Free Press, 1955), p. 1.

13. Ibid., p. 1.

14. Ibid., p. 23.

15. Ibid., pp. 30 ff.; Rossi notes the fact that higher status groups show more sociability which offsets some of this trend, though their contacts are nonlocal.

16. 1924, op. cit., p. 211; *Spring* 1926, op. cit., p. 144; 1935, op. cit., p. 53; *The Effective City Church* by Murray Leiffer (Nashville: Abingdon-Cokesbury, 1949), pp. 147 ff.

17. *The American City and Its Church* by Samuel C. Kinchloe (New York: The Friendship Press, 1938), p. 118.

18. The author is indebted to Peter Rossi, op. cit., p. 59 f., for his analysis of organizational adjustment to residential mobility.

19. For a discussion of the Protestant emphasis on the congregational community see *A Theology of the Laity* by Hendrik Kraemer, op. cit.

20. *Social Relations in the Urban Parish* by Joseph Fichter, S.J. (Chicago: University of Chicago Press, 1954), p. 188.

21. *The Living and the Dead*, op. cit., pp. 240 ff.

22. The author is indebted to Dr. Paul Pruyser of the Menninger Clinic for the suggestion that congregational drudgery may be a way of handling guilt. The present writer, of course, takes full responsibility for the present application of this notion to the organization church.

23. A term used by Dietrich Bonhoeffer in *The Cost of Discipleship*, Rev. Ed. (London: SCM Press, 1959), pp. 35–47.

24. "The Major Dimensions of Religious Membership" by Yoshio Fukuyama (unpublished Ph.D. dissertation, University of Chicago, 1960).

25. 1948, op. cit., p. 185.

26. *Collective* is used here with some negative connotation; that is, it implies the transformation of an organization whose nature is to

fulfill some purpose beyond itself into *an end in itself*. It is this aspect of the "collective society"—the transmutation of a *means* for order and peace into the *end*—which makes it distasteful to the liberal tradition. Man is thus conceived as the servant of society. The organization church could become an instrument of mission, but by identifying itself with a particular social class it drains the energy and funds of the members into its own perpetuation. The middle-class White congregation that rejects desegregation because it might jeopardize the church is an instance of the "collective" mind, which prevents the Church from becoming a medium of reconciliation. There is a necessary tension between organizational goals and the efforts of a membership to maintain a continuing identity, since the fulfillment of a task can strain and even disrupt the relations between members. When continuity as a community and fulfillment of a mission cease to create strains because the mission has been assimilated to the maintenance of identity (mission as co-optation), the church has become a collective. The contrast between collectivism and individualism is apropos, since the collective transforms all but its own perpetuation into means, the individual into an expendable part; but the contrast drawn here is between the church in its communal, organizational processes and the church as a collective. For another use of the term collectivity, see *The Social System* by Talcott Parsons (Glencoe, Ill.: The Free Press, 1951) p. 39, where the term is used neutrally to designate a system of interactive roles, much as association was used in late medieval theory.

CHAPTER FIVE

1. *Race and Nationality in American Life* by Oscar Handlin (New York: Doubleday Anchor Books, 1957); Will Herberg, op. cit., Chapters II and III.
2. In H. Paul Douglass's studies, the Southern and Eastern European churches developed diversified programs, but these did not follow the pattern of organization churches.
3. See *The Uprooted*, op. cit.; *The Polish Peasant in Europe and America* by W. I. Thomas and Florian Znaniecki (Boston: Gor-

ham Press, 1920); W. Lloyd Warner and Leo Strole, op. cit., Chapter I.

4. *The Ghetto* by Louis Wirth, op. cit., contains a brilliant analysis of this struggle between two worlds.

5. *The American People in the Twentieth Century* by Oscar Handlin (Cambridge, Mass.: Harvard University Press, 1954), pp. 221–22, cited by Joseph Kahl, op. cit., p. 233.

6. 1926, op. cit., p. 196.

7. R. W. Sanderson refers to this communal bond as clannishness; it continues to characterize ethnic churches. See 1932, op. cit., pp. 168 f.; *The Social Sources of Denominationalism* by H. Richard Niebuhr (Hamden, Conn.: The Shoe String Press, Reprinted 1954), Chapter Eight, which stresses both the rigidity in controversy and accommodation of ethnic churches.

8. Some ethnic churches refused to adapt and alienated upwardly mobile members (1932, op. cit., p. 166), but the self-contained, internally oriented churches in H. Paul Douglass's study, comprising one fourth of his sample (1926, op. cit., Table LXXI, p. 301), were largely ethnic churches which moved to better areas and became organization churches.

9. Will Herberg referred to this transformation in private discussion with the writer when he pointed out that religion was a part of ethnicity in the first generation, whereas ethnicity is a part of religion in the third generation.

10. Gunnar Myrdal, op. cit., Chapter 40; *The Social Sources of Denominationalism* by H. R. Niebuhr, op. cit., Chapter Nine; *The Negro in the United States* by E. F. Frazier, op. cit., Chapter XIV, esp. p. 347; *The Racial Problem in Christian Perspective* by Kyle Haselden (New York: Harper, 1959), Chapter 1.

11. *Black Metropolis* by St. Clair Drake and Horace R. Cayton (New York: Harcourt, Brace, 1945), Chapters 2 and 3; Gunnar Myrdal, op. cit., Chapters 28–32.

12. *Ambivalence* is intended to suggest here a simultaneously positive and negative movement. This is illustrated in reactions to colors by Negro adolescents—first rejecting black as distasteful, then White. Their rejection of black is a reflection of White attitudes internalized by the adolescent (White-positive, Negro-negative); their rejection of White is an internalization of the Negro, mi-

nority attitude (Negro-positive, White-negative). See the summary
of this study and of research in the field of prejudice in *The Nature of Prejudice* by Gordon W. Allport (Boston: Beacon Press,
1954), pp. 152, 302 ff.; see also *Segregation and Desegregation* by
Melvin M. Tumin (New York: Anti-Defamation League of B'nai
B'rith, 1957) for a summary of research.

13. This interpretation of the Negro community as internally divided,
since it contradicts by its nature the ethos of the American community, is implicit in Gunnar Myrdal's monumental work, *An
American Dilemma*, op. cit., and is expressed in the ambivalence
of the Negro upper classes as described in *Black Bourgeoisie* by
E. F. Frazier (Glencoe, Ill.: The Free Press, 1957). The notion
of a caste system in America expresses the involuntary and even
paradoxical character of a "Negro community" in the United
States; see "Introduction: Deep South—A Social Anthropological
Study of Caste and Class" by W. Lloyd Warner; Chapter 1 of
Deep South by Allison Davis, Burleigh B. Gardner, and Mary R.
Gardner (Chicago: University of Chicago Press, 1941).

14. St. Clair Drake and Horace R. Cayton, op. cit., Chapter 2 and
esp. pp. 202 ff.; for a full analysis of ghettos and their expansion
in Chicago, see *The Negro Population of Chicago* by Otis D. Duncan and Beverly Duncan (Chicago: University of Chicago Press,
1957).

15. St. Clair Drake and Horace R. Cayton, op. cit., Chapter 9.

16. This is the picture of the model Negro church in the urban ghetto
of the 1920s and should not be confused with the upper-class
churches of the established and cultivated Negro communities.
See E. F. Frazier, *The Negro in the United States*, pp. 349 f.; note
that in 1936 seven eighths of Negro churches were in the rural
and urban South, and (p. 355) that of 500 Negro churches in a
northern area 75 per cent were storefronts. This picture of imposed
poverty and segregation we shall discuss further in the analysis of
sectarianism.

17. See St. Clair Drake and Horace R. Cayton, op. cit., Chapter 6,
for a discussion of these problems among the lower classes and
the widespread resentment of the churches.

18. H. Paul Douglass had to treat his small sample of Negro churches
as widely variant in elaboration since their organizations diverged
sharply from the White churches, See 1926, op. cit., pp. 196, 273;

see also B. E. Mays and J. W. Nicholson, op. cit., pp. 119–22, 155.

19. E. F. Frazier, *The Negro in the United States*, pp. 349 f.

20. E. F. Frazier, *Black Bourgeoisie*, op. cit., pp. 25 f., 89 f., 228 f.

21. St. Clair Drake and Horace R. Cayton, op. cit., Chapter 7 and esp. p. 678.

22. Ibid., p. 678.

23. Ibid., pp. 679–82.

24. Ibid., pp. 537 ff., and *The Negro in the United States* by E. F. Frazier, op. cit., p. 354.

25. E. F. Frazier has accented this note in his discussions of the Negro bourgeoisie.

26. The literature on sects and sectarianism is rich and extensive. See *Small Sects in America* by Elmer T. Clark (New York: Abingdon-Cokesbury Press, 1949); *The Social Sources of Denominationalism* by H. Richard Niebuhr, op. cit., Chapters II and III; *Millhands and Preachers* by Liston Pope (New Haven: Yale University Press, 1942); *Religion in Crisis and Custom* by Anton Boisen (New York: Harper, 1945).

27. The significance of this type of shock in the emergence of sects in the city was stressed by John B. Holt in his article "Holiness Religion, Cultural Shock, and Social Reorganization" in American Sociological Review, Vol. 5, No. 5, Oct. 1940, pp. 740–47. For analysis of lower lower-class experiences, see *Family and Class Dynamics in Mental Illness* by Jerome K. Myers and Bertram H. Roberts (New York: John Wiley, 1959), esp. Chapter 4.

28. The terms "insider" and "outsider" are used to discriminate established churches (middle-class) from sectarian churches in *As You Sow* by Walter Goldschmidt (New York: Harcourt, Brace, 1947). See esp. Table 24, p. 136.

29. Contrast, for example, the Norwegian sectarian group in *Democracy in Jonesville* by W. Lloyd Warner et al., op. cit., Chapter 11, with some of the cult groups in *These Also Believe* by Charles J. Braden (New York: Macmillan, 1949).

30. Everett L. Perry, op. cit.

31. "The Sectarian Black and White World" by Calvin Redikop (unpublished Ph.D. dissertation, University of Chicago, 1959).

32. "Ethnics" by E. K. Francis in *Race*, edited by E. T. Thompson and E. C. Hughes (Glencoe, Ill., The Free Press, 1938), pp. 71–79.

33. J. K. Myers and B. H. Roberts, op. cit., p. 49; "The Motivation of the Underprivileged Worker" by Allison Davis in *Industry and Society*, edited by William Foote Whyte (New York and London: McGraw-Hill, 1946), Chapter V.
34. This is not a value judgment on the sects but an analysis in terms of social class. The sect approximates the early Christian church and has a significant place in the Christian tradition. See "The Challenge of the Sects" by H. P. Van Dusen in *Christianity and Crisis*, 1958, pp. 103 f.
35. E. F. Frazier, *The Negro in the United States*, pp. 334–66.
36. *The Protestant Ethic and the Spirit of Capitalism* by Max Weber, translated by Talcott Parsons (London: George Allen & Unwin, Ltd., 1930), pp. 174 f.; E. R. Wickham, op. cit., Chapter 4.
37. Walter Goldschmidt, op. cit., describes this process in an outsider church; see also "The Sociology of Secularization" by H. W. Pfautz in *American Journal of Sociology*, Vol. 61, Sept. 1955, pp. 121 ff.; see also "The Church of God" by Val Clear (unpublished Ph.D. dissertation, University of Chicago, 1953).
38. *1948*, op. cit., pp. 158–61.
39. *Social Class and Mental Illness* by A. B. Hollingshead and F. C. Redlich (New York: John Wiley, 1958); J. K. Myers and B. D. Roberts, op. cit.

CHAPTER SIX

1. *Evanston Speaks*: reports from the second assembly of the World Council of Churches (New York: World Council of Churches, 1954), p. 27. For a discussion of this theme, see *Foundations of the Responsible Society* by Walter G. Muelder (Nashville, Tenn.: Abingdon Press, 1959), esp. pp. 18 ff.
2. *Christ and Culture* by H. R. Niebuhr (New York: Harper, 1951), pp. 46 ff., identifies the radical commandment of love in the First Epistle of John with a "Christ against culture" motif, and yet the radical love motif underlies all Christian ethics. However legitimate this identification, embodiments of Christianity have never viewed the love commandment as optional, although some have limited the scope of its application and others have confined its bearing to an in-group. For an exposition of the generality of this

commandment in Christian ethics, see "The New Look in Christian Ethics" by Joseph Fletcher, *Harvard Divinity Bulletin*, Oct. 1959. pp. 7–18.

3. *English Villagers of the Thirteenth Century* by George C. Homans (Cambridge, Mass.: Harvard University Press, 1941).

4. The segregation of spheres of life is treated analytically in "A Revised Analytical Approach to the Theory of Social Stratification" by Talcott Parsons in *Class, Status and Power*, edited by Reinhard Bendix and S. M. Lipset (Glencoe, Ill.: The Free Press, 1953), pp. 92–128 and esp. pp. 116 ff. The segregation of these contexts of work, shopping, and residential areas are empirically demonstrated in a study of the determination of attitudes toward Negroes by the collective structures in these different spheres; see "Collective Factors in Race Relations" by Dietrich Reitzes (unpublished Ph.D. dissertation, University of Chicago, 1950).

5. Annual values of new construction have been mounting steadily, exceeding $800,000,000 in 1958; for figures prior to 1958 see *Yearbook of American Churches, 1958*, op. cit., p. 293. Most of this construction is in suburban areas, but even at increased rates the present pattern of congregations and ministries will fall far short of needs. Even if the pattern were good, which it is not since it confines the churches to private life, it could not be sustained.

6. This fact was brought out in the analysis of the clearly conceived plan for Greater Indianapolis developed by Fred Michel and presented at the consultation on Urban Planning and Research, Indianapolis, Nov. 1959.

7. Dietrich Reitzes, op. cit., has presented data for a residential neighborhood, shopping area, and industrial union where the same people entertained different attitudes, moral norms, and values. In a mass society, chambers of commerce, property owners associations, labor unions, and the like, set the standards for particular contexts. Moral norms are shaped by these standards. A similar phenomenon was demonstrated in the effect of a standard of mixed Negro-White occupancy set by public authority and altered prejudice; see *Interracial Housing* by Morton Deutsch and Mary E. Collins (Minneapolis: University of Minnesota Press, 1951), esp. Appendix A.

8. "The Second Children's Crusade" (subtitled "overemphasis on the family in suburbia's churches is basically subversive of the Chris-

tian mission") by Peter L. Berger in *Christian Century*, Dec. 2, 1959, pp. 399 f., expresses a sharp awareness of this privatization of religiousness to child care and emotional problems. The basic issue, however, is a deformation of religiousness which requires a reformation. This deformation can be pointed up by exhortation to mission, but it will be altered only by basic structural change. "The Test of the Christian Faith Today" by Reinhold Niebuhr in *Christian Century*, Oct. 28, 1959, pp. 1239 ff., suggests a middle ground which accepts the collective structures as now too complex for theological appraisal and stresses the privatized impact of religiousness with an upholding of the transcendent majesty of God's purposes. This is full circle in Reformation theology, since it is a return to Martin Luther's "two kingdoms theory" in the context of a technological society. Although this alternative is rejected here, it is a serious alternative and is stated with penetration by Niebuhr.

9. *Church and People in an Industrial City* by E. R. Wickham, op. cit., esp. Chapter VI.

10. The data for this interpretation has been drawn from the following sources: "The Parish Church and Delinquency" by Kilmer Myers from *Christianity and Crisis*, 1958; *Light the Dark Streets* by Kilmer Myers (Greenwich, Conn.: Seabury Press, 1958); "The Local Church and Juvenile Delinquency" by J. Archie Hargreaves from *Christianity and Crisis*, Jan. 1958; "The Parish and Delinquency: East Harlem" by George Todd from *Christianity and Crisis*; correspondence Sept. 1958; "The Inner City Ministry as I See It," from *The City Church* by J. Archie Hargreaves, Jan.–Feb. 1957, p. 10 ff.; "Proposal for a Demonstration Project," mimeographed plans for Nazarene Congregational Church in Brooklyn, N.Y.; Pierre Delattre, "San Francisco–North Beach Project," mimeographed letter, April 13, 1958; Reverend and Mrs. Michael Hamilton, "Ministry to the Southern Mountaineer," mimeographed report, 1958; "The Problem of a Christian Witness in Greenwich Village," mimeographed statement by Staff of Judson Church, N.Y., May 1958. Don Benedict, Robert Manly, and others in the Inner City Parish of Cleveland have formed a pattern of organization which gives local flexibility and organized power. See also Ernest Southcott *The Parish Comes Alive* (New York: Morehouse-Gorham, 1956), for work in Halton Parish, Leeds, England.

11. There is an example of this in the team ministry in Christ Church, Bloomfield Hills, Mich., where a pattern of house churches has been set up. Other such experiments are being developed or considered, among them one by Robert L. Green and Kenneth Robinson in Wilton, Conn.
12. Kilmer Myers, "The Parish Church and Delinquency," op. cit., p. 33.
13. J. Archie Hargreaves in *The City Church*, op. cit., p. 10.
14. Reverend and Mrs. Michael Hamilton, op. cit., p. 24.
15. Judson Memorial Staff, op. cit., p. 6.
16. George Todd, op. cit.
17. *The Shook-Up Generation* by Harrison E. Salisbury (New York: Harper, 1958).
18. Robert Spike in *Religion and Social Work*, edited by F. Ernest Johnson (New York: Harper, 1956).
19. Kilmer Myers, *Light the Dark Streets*.
20. See discussion by Bishop James Pike of San Francisco, "That They May Be One," *Christian Century*, Jan. 13, 1960.
21. Note the development of the household church in Ernest Southcott, op. cit.
22. A sector ministry would require a *church week*, similar to the German *Kirchentag*, to build the total life of the sector.
23. R. C. Angell, *Free Society and Moral Crisis*, op. cit., p. 229.
24. Various ministries to hospital, industrial, political, and university groups have emerged in the last generation. The most developed ministry to industry is in Sheffield, England, although the Detroit Industrial Mission has already demonstrated the need for such a ministry in the United States. For a statement of the need for such ministries, see E. R. Wickham, *Church and People in an Industrial City*, op. cit., Chapter VI.
25. For a discussion of various centers of renewal, see *Signs of Renewal*, Department on the Laity, World Council of Churches.
26. There are various ways to formulate this emerging crisis. A breakdown of communication under the pressures and complexities of metropolitan life is a good approximation. See *Metropolis in Ferment*, special issue of *The Annals*, Vol. 314, Nov. 1957, esp. pp. 57–65 and 123–46.
27. *The Household of Faith* by Ralph Morton (Glasgow: The Iona Community, 1958), esp. Part II.

CHAPTER SEVEN

1. *Juvenile Delinquency* by Joseph D. Lohman (Cook County, Ill.: Office of the Sheriff, 1957), p. 14.
2. See A. B. Hollingshead and F. C. Redlich, op. cit., for an analysis of the withdrawal trends in the "untouchable" segments of the city; see also J. K. Myers and B. H. Roberts, op. cit., pp. 253–58.
3. "Metropolitan Organization" by Luther Gulick in *Metropolis in Ferment*, special issue of *The Annals*, op. cit., pp. 57–65; for a statement of the role of planning in the churches, see *Urban Church Planning* by Walter Kloetzli and Arthur Hillman (Philadelphia: Muhlenberg Press, 1958), esp. Chapters 5 and 10.
4. *Popular Religion* by Louis Schneider and Sanford M. Dornbusch (Chicago: University of Chicago Press, 1958) includes a discussion of this equation of individual virtue with social health in popular religious books, pp. 96 ff.
5. Two of the best discussions of Protestantism which take this approach are *Protestant–Catholic–Jew* by Will Herberg, op. cit., and *The Shape of American Religion* by Martin E. Marty (New York: Harper, 1959).
6. For a statement of the case against institutionalization, see *The Kingdom of God in America* by H. Richard Niebuhr (New York: Harper, Torch Books, 1937 and 1959), Chapter V; for a more balanced statement by the same author, see *The Purpose of the Church and Its Ministry*, op. cit., pp. 21 ff. Paul Tillich treats this theme in "The Protestant Principle and the Proletarian Situation," Chapter XI of *The Protestant Era* (Chicago: University of Chicago Press, 1948), esp. pp. 162 f. Even H. Paul Douglass considers the organization a non-theological aspect of the Church; see 1935, op. cit., pp. 4 ff.
7. See A. B. Hollingshead and F. C. Redlich, op. cit., esp. pp. 223–32 for the trends to psychoses in the lower classes and neuroses in the middle and upper classes.
8. Ibid., for a discussion of the middle-class style of psychiatric practice which has close parallels in the style of the organization church, pp. 344 ff.; Will Herberg, op. cit., p. 90, notes the alienation of lower-class groups, although he is principally concerned

with integration to the basic values of the American way of life.

9. See the discussion of collective structures in Dietrich Reitzes, op. cit. For a recent example of the collective determination of moral standards which operate in terms of interests rather than individual and moral attitudes, see *Last Man In, Racial Access to Union Power* by Scott Greer (Glencoe, Ill.: The Free Press, 1959).

10. Hannah Arendt, op. cit., p. 61, summarizes the complexity of this situation, when the private sphere—economy and necessity—replaces the public sphere and both become submerged in conformity to the social sphere. See also a discussion of the preoccupation with intimacy in *Love and Conflict* by Gibson Winter (Garden City, N.Y.: Doubleday, 1958), Chapter 8.

11. A *Theology of the Laity* by Hendrik Kraemer, op. cit., pp. 136 ff., for a discussion of the Church, as mission and servantship.

12. "Toward a Metropolitan Meaning of Community" by Perry L. Norton, reprinted from *City Church*, Division of Home Missions, National Council of Churches of Christ in the U.S.A., New York 27, N.Y.

13. An increasing number of suburban laymen are joining central city churches in order to share their ministry; the principle of the sector ministry is to integrate this responsibility rather than to exclude laymen from responsibility for the whole city.

14. From a different perspective, this uneasiness about concern with unity was voiced in *The Great Tradition of the American Churches* by Winthrop S. Hudson (New York: Harper, 1953), pp. 254 ff.

15. *Ephesians* 1:22 f.: "And hath put all things under his feet, and gave him to be the head over all things to the Church, which is his body, the fullness of him that filleth all in all." (R.S.V.) Participation in the Church means sharing in the infinite richness of the grace of God; through the Church, Christ's Lordship is manifest over all creation. See also *Colossians* 2:9 f.; *The Interpreter's Bible* (Nashville, Tenn.: Abingdon Press, 1953), Vol. X, p. 637; "L'Épître de Saint Paul aux Ephesiens" by Charles Masson in *Commentaire du Nouveau Testament*, IX (Neuchatel: Delachaux, Niestlé, 1953) pp. 155 f. The pleroma of Christ means full communion with God through Christ in the Church, and the fulfillment of the divine purpose to unite all things—the *whole* creation —in Him.

Index

Exclusiveness: ethnic, 66; in local communal groupings, 73–74

Exodus (Protestant), 39–58, 105, 136, 137, 150, 161; from central city, 34–35; emergence of new Protestantism, 57–58; identification with new middle class, 49–57; importance of, 56; index of growth, 42

Experimental ministries, 139, 140–41, 142, 143–44, 147

"Exploding" metropolis, 15

External upgrading, 42

Faith, 69, 70, 134; defined, 136–37; fullness of, 176; in sects, 124

Fellowship, 75, 77–78, 102; of churches, 61; by likeness, 75

Fichter, Joseph, 90

Finance, 144

Folk religion, 114, 116

Foreign-born, Protestant congregations of, 106. See also Ethnic churches

Forgiveness, 97

Founding Fathers, 15

France, 50

Frazier, E. Franklin, 114

Frontier Evangelism Associates, 11

Fukuyama, Yoshio, 99

Fund raising, in organization church, 94–96

Germany, 154

Ghetto, The, 23

Gift exchanges, 94–96

Gold Coast and the Slum, The, 18

Gospel, 134, 163

Grace, "cheap," 97

Greenwich Village, 141

Grodzins, Morton, 19–20

Guilt feelings, 97, 98

Hamilton, Michael, 141

Hargreaves, J. Archie, 141

Hawley, Amos, 17

Herberg, Will, 27

Heterogeneity, of metropolitan areas, 66

Homogeneity: of churches, 66; economic level and, 68; ethnic, 66; of residential areas, 65–66

Hospitals, ministries to, 153–54, 168

"House churches," 102

Identity: personal, 77; religious, 172; search for, 75, 76; sectarian, 119, 120–22, 124; social, 102, 103, 107, 113, 119, 124, 142, 158, 165

Immigrant, 106 ff.; life, 106–7

Immigration, 18, 42, 47, 106

Impersonality, of organization church, 92

Impersonal interdependence, 27–28, 73–74, 161

Incarnation, doctrine of, 141

Industrialization, 15–16, 42, 165; effect on Protestant responsibility, 132

Industrial Revolution, 51–52, 60

Industrial society: segregation of spheres of life in, 132; sickness of, 166

Industry, mission to, 157

In-migration, 42; Negroes, 44, 48; rural White Protestants, 43; Whites, 48

Inner city: and the inclusive community, 140–51; diversification in, 141; life in, 119 ff.; ministry to, 139–40, problems of, 144; test of inclusive church, 139

Insulated community, 23, 25–26, 27

Insulated congregation, 170

Integrated churches, 117, 174

Integration, 44, 46, 158; church, 117, 174; economic, 62–71, 73; racial, in residential areas, 135–36

Intellectual style church membership, 99

Interdenominational union, 37

Interdependence: denial of, 78; essence of humanity, 78; impersonality of, 27–28, 73–74, 161; in metropolis, 20–21, 29

Interfaith communication, 36, 37

Internal upgrading, 42

Residential areas, 81; homogeneity of, 65–66; productive society and, 81. *See* Back of the Yards Council

Residential association, 64–65, 74, 75

Residential community, 25; history of, 132; segregated context of, 156

Residential exclusion, 74

Residential mobility, 70; in metropolis, 87–88; organization church resistance to, 98; Protestantism and, 88–89; Roman Catholicism and, 90

Residential patterns, in metropolis, 19–20

Responsibility: of church, 129–30, 131; context of, 130; Protestant, 33, 132; public, church and, 131; religious, 161–62

Resurrection, 163

Retreats, 168

Reveille for Radicals, 26

Roman Catholic church: client-oriented organization, 89–90; congregations, 106; impersonality of, 71; parishes, and residential mobility, 90; priesthood, 89

Roman Catholic development, 10

Roman Catholic immigrations, 42–43, 47

Roman Catholicism, 58, 100

Rome, 62

Rossi, Peter, 87–88, 89

Rural churches, organization pattern, 86

Sacraments, 168

St. Augustine, 49–50

St. Louis, Missouri, 51, 99; Protestantism in, 43

St. Paul, 61

St. Peter, 61

Salisbury, Harrison, 143

Salvation, 102; by works, 101

San Francisco, Episcopal Diocese, 147

Satellite areas, 18, 19; church concentration on, 32; ministry to, 149

Satellite communities, 18, 21

Scott, Robert, 11

Scriptures, 140

Sect, 165; characteristics of, 119; denomination and, 122–23; introversion of, 124; metropolitan, 122; missionary work of, 124; and organization church, 122. *See also* Sectarian identity

Sectarian community, 123

Sectarian congregations, transition of, 125, *chart*, 126

Sectarian groups, common element in, 118

Sectarian identity, 119, 120–22, 124

Sectarian religiousness, 118–25

Sector ministries, 145–46, 147–48, 149, 151, 152, 153, 154, 155, 157, 158, 170, 171; purpose of, 150

Secularization, 124

Segregation, 34, 128; of consuming and producing spheres, 156, 158

Separation, residence from work, 60, 63, 65, 67, 81, 133

Sheffield, England, 157

"Sit-in" strikes, 1960, 113

Social classes, schism in metropolitan life, 20

Social identity, 102, 103, 158, 165; ethnic community, 107; Negro, 113; religious ground of, 142; sect and, 119; sectarian and, 124

Social mobility, foreign-born and, 110–11

Social organization in metropolis, 20 ff., 29

Social responsibility, of churches, 136

Sociability, in mobile areas, 88

South, the: ante-bellum, 64; caste system, 114; post-bellum, 64; residence in, 63

South Africa, 78

Southern Europeans, congregations of, 108–9

Spheres, diversity of in contemporary life, 153

Spike, Robert, 143

Spirituality, 163

Springfield, Massachusetts, 99

Stability: need for, 75; struggle for, 34–35

Standard metropolitan areas, 16. *See* Metropolitan areas

Status panic, 29, 34, 157

Suburban congregations, ministry to inner city, 144

Suburbs, churches success in, 15

Sweden, 50

Swedish Lutheranism, 66

Symbols, 168

T'Hooft, Visser, 37

Tip-point, 46, 47; defined, 45

Todd, George, 142, 143

Traditionalism, and ethnic church, 106

United Church of Christ, 32

United States: Christianity, problem of, 138; irreligiousness in, 15; metropolitan areas, number of, 16; metropolitan domination in, 17; metropolis, importance of, 15; Protestantism in, 131; religiousness in, 15; urbanization of, 15–16

United States Supreme Court, 19, 45

Universities, ministries to, 153–54, 168

Upgrading, major denominations, 48

Urban blight, 9, 10, 28, 29, 46, 70, 161, 162

Urban churches: activities, 84–87; government by committees, 85–86; rural, differences in organization, 84; special ministries, 85

Urban expansion, 39

Urban interdependence, 21 ff.

Urbanism, 84

Urbanization: and Christianity, 50; churches and, 30; of United States, 15–16

Van Buren, Paul, 11

Walker, John, 11

Warner, William Lloyd, 83, 94

Waycross, 168

Western Europe, 50, 51; Christianity in, 57–58

"White-collar pyramid," 52

White collar workers, 39. *See* Middle class

White culture, Negro identification with, 115

White Protestantism, 39, 40; branches, 31; and desegregation, 76; Negro threat to, 44; retreat from Negroes, 45 ff.

White Protestants, 39, 40; congregations, 41 ff.; rural, in-migrations of, 43; upgrading of, 40

Whites: Negro schism, 20; Protestantism and, 31; residential pattern in metropolis, 24

Wickham, E. R., 138

Wicklein, John, 33

Wirth, Louis, 23–24

Working classes: disengagement of Christianity from, 49; Protestant churches and, 41

World Council of Churches, 129

World War I, 16, 18, 44, 85

World War II, 22, 44, 101, 135, 156

Worship, 148–49. *See also* Public worship

Yankee City, 83, 94

Zorbaugh, Harvey, 18